# THE COMPLETE GUIDE TO

# THE

# REVOLUTIONARY WAR

## JULIA GARSTECKI

**Sandy Creek**
NEW YORK

An Imprint of Sterling Publishing Co., Inc.
1166 Avenue of the Americas
New York, NY 10036

SANDY CREEK and the distinctive SANDY CREEK logo
are registered trademarks of Barnes & Noble, Inc.

Text © 2016 by QEB Publishing, Inc.
Illustrations © 2016 by QEB Publishing, Inc.

All rights reserved. No part of this publication
may be reproduced, stored in a retrieval system
or transmitted in any form or by any means
(including electronic, mechanical, photocopying,
recording, or otherwise) without prior written
permission from the publisher.

ISBN 978-1-4351-6359-1

Manufactured in Guangdong, China
Lot #:
2  4  6  8  10  9  7  5  3  1
08/16

www.sterlingpublishing.com

**Picture credits**
(t=top, b=bottom, l=left, r=right, c=center, fc=front cover,
bc=back cover)

All images are public domain unless stated.

**Ahodges7**
102bl creative commons attribution

**Alamy**
52–53 508 Collection, 106–107 Classic Image, 102–103
Glasshouse Images, 62–63, 72–73, 76–77, 84–85, 88–89,
110–111, 112–113, 118–119, 128tr Granger, NYC, 22–23
Lebrecht Music and Arts Photo Library, 94–95 Niday
Picture Library, 18–19, 44–45, 45bl, 48–49, 49cr, 68br,
78–79, 82–83, 86–87, 100–101, 104–105, 108–109 North
Wind Picture Archives, 104bl The Art Archive.

**Anthony22**
73cr creative commons attribution

**Daderot**
136br creative commons attribution

**Dreamstime.com**
139tr and c Agnieszka Murphy, 60–61, 83bl Alexandre
Fagundes De Fagundes, 7tr , 68–69 American spirit, 40–41
Bambi L. Dingman, 61tl David Dredeson, 27tc F11photo,
17cr Foto21293, 14bl, 91tr Georgios Kollidas, 8br Jennifer
Thompson, 50–51 J. Paul Grow, 32–33, 134–135 Jorge
Salcedo, 36tr Ken Backer, 70–71 Kongomonkey, 93b Lee
Snider, 37bl Mb2006, 16cl Nilabarathi, 17tc Oliver Nowak,
95tr, 137cr Olivier Le Queinec, 39bl Ritu Jethani, 108bl
Scott Anderson, 24bl Sean Pavone, 138–139 Splosh, 61br
trekandshoot, 58–59 Warasit Phothisuk, 135bl Washington
Imaging, 30–31 Zrfphoto

**Samuel, David**
124bl creative commons attribution

**Sdwelch1031**
87tr creative commons attribution

**Wade, Matt**
136–137 creative commons attribution

**Wellcome Trust**
17br creative commons attribution

**Yale Centre for British Art**
29cr creative commons attribution

# THE COMPLETE GUIDE TO

# THE
# REVOLUTIONARY
# WAR

## JULIA GARSTECKI

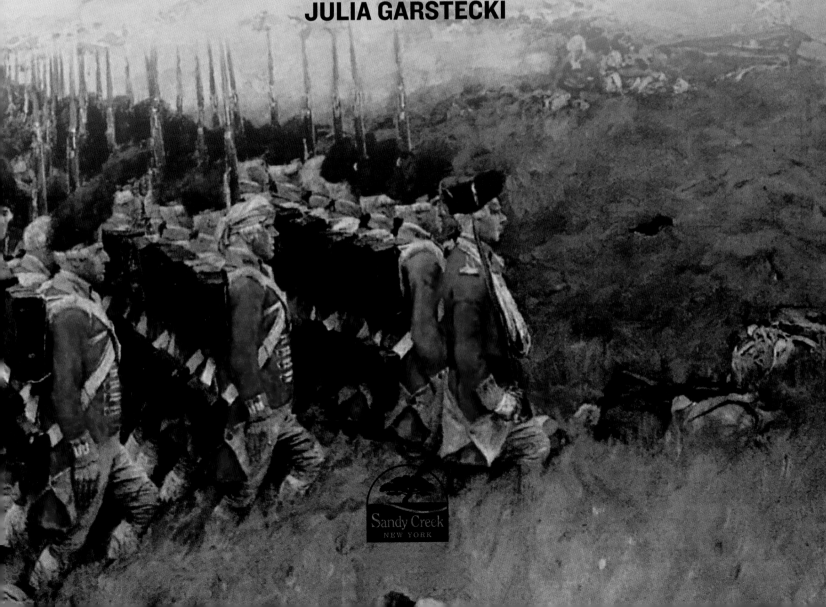

Sandy Creek
NEW YORK

# CONTENTS

Words in **bold** are explained in the Glossary on page 140.

# INTRODUCTION

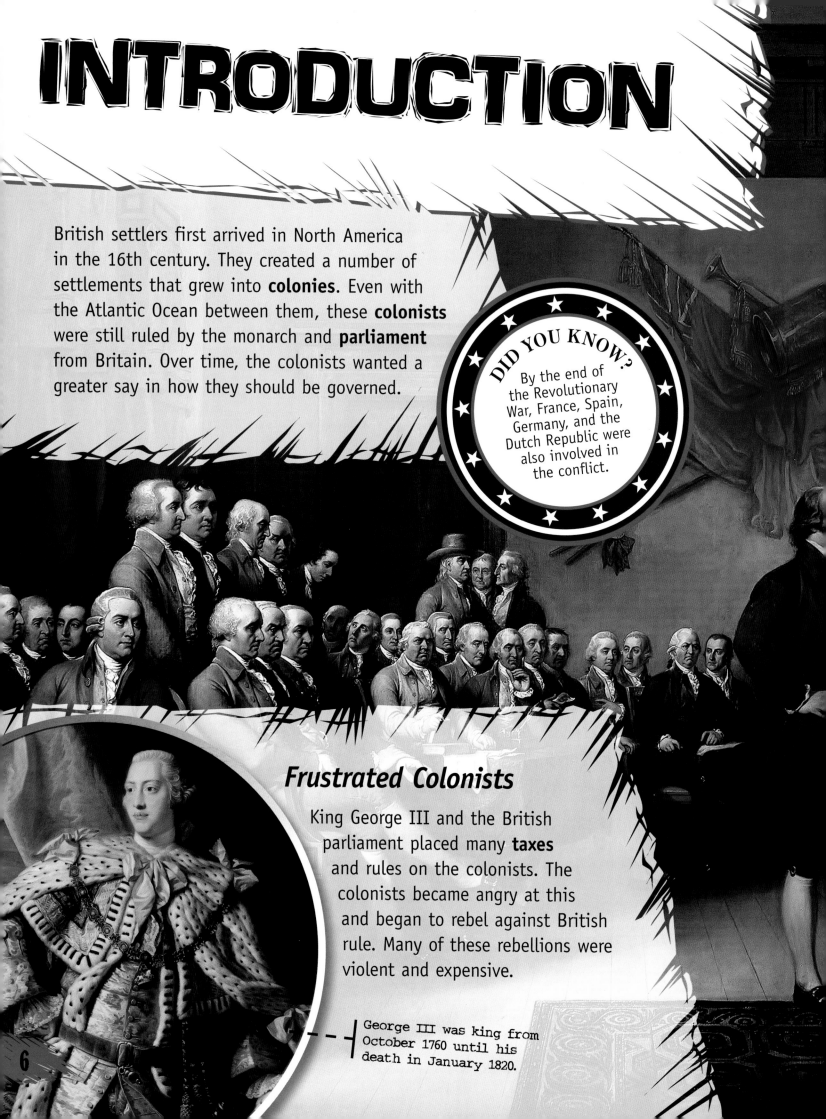

British settlers first arrived in North America in the 16th century. They created a number of settlements that grew into **colonies**. Even with the Atlantic Ocean between them, these **colonists** were still ruled by the monarch and **parliament** from Britain. Over time, the colonists wanted a greater say in how they should be governed.

## Frustrated Colonists

King George III and the British parliament placed many **taxes** and rules on the colonists. The colonists became angry at this and began to rebel against British rule. Many of these rebellions were violent and expensive.

George III was king from October 1760 until his death in January 1820.

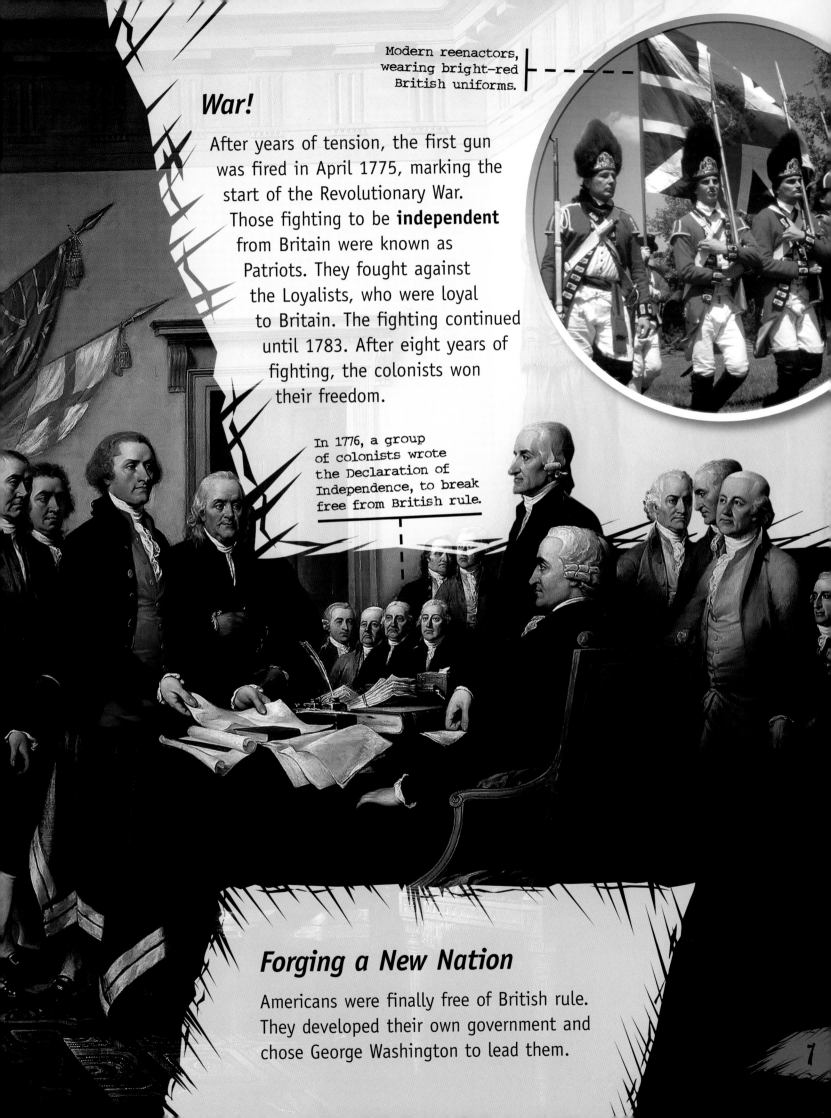

# War!

After years of tension, the first gun was fired in April 1775, marking the start of the Revolutionary War. Those fighting to be **independent** from Britain were known as Patriots. They fought against the Loyalists, who were loyal to Britain. The fighting continued until 1783. After eight years of fighting, the colonists won their freedom.

In 1776, a group of colonists wrote the Declaration of Independence, to break free from British rule.

# Forging a New Nation

Americans were finally free of British rule. They developed their own government and chose George Washington to lead them.

# SETTLEMENT OF AMERICA

The first peoples to settle in North America probably came from Siberia in 30,000–11,000 BCE. These **nomadic** hunters would have followed the animals that came to North America. Many groups of people formed tribes and civilizations throughout North and South America, creating their own languages and ways of living.

The first people probably crossed Beringia, a land bridge between Siberia and Alaska that no longer exists.

Siberia

Alaska

KEY
— Present coastline
 Land bridge

## Finding the New World

In 1492, European adventurers found North and South America and began to explore it. The Spanish established the first European settlement in Florida in 1565. France settled on land in the north, in Canada. The first British settlement was in Jamestown, Virginia, in 1607. By 1750, Dutch, Swedish, and German settlements dotted the North American coastline as well.

A recreation of the settlement at Jamestown, Virginia.

## Slaves

Between 1492 and 1770, some 10 million slaves were brought to North and South America. By 1775, about 260,000 slaves had been brought to the North American colonies. They were forced to clear fields and look after crops. Most were treated harshly.

Spanish explorer Christopher Columbus was the first European to reach the Americas in 1492.

Slaves were brought from Africa in terrible conditions aboard slave ships.

PLAN OF LOWER DECK WITH THE STOWAGE OF 292 SLAVES
130 OF THESE BEING STOWED UNDER THE SHELVES AS SHEWN IN FIGURE B & FIGURE 5.

DID YOU KNOW?
There were many distinct groups of Native Americans. Some, like the Iroquois and Algonquin, spent years at war with each other.

# THE FRENCH AND INDIAN WAR

By the middle of the 18th century, French settlers living near the Great Lakes were trapping large amounts of fur to sell around the world. However, this brought them into conflict with the local Iroquois people and the two groups soon started fighting. To help them fight the Iroquois, the French sought the help of other native people, such as the Algonquin and the Huron.

Iroquois people trading goods with western settlers in the 17th century.

## DID YOU KNOW?

At the end of the war, France lost all of Canada and gave Louisiana to Spain. The French were very upset, and eager to regain this territory.

## Challenging the French

The British saw a chance to undermine the French in North America and take their trade and land. The British parliament sent soldiers to fight against the French, starting the French and Indian War.

Native Americans attack British troops and civilians during the French and Indian War.

## The British Win

The war lasted from 1754 to 1763, with the British eventually winning. However, training and maintaining soldiers for such a long time was very costly. The British government also knew it needed to keep troops in America to protect its colonies in any future wars. This meant they needed even more money. To raise funds, the government would have to tax the colonists. This greatly upset the colonists and eventually led to revolution.

Great Lakes

Atlantic Ocean

Mississippi River

**KEY**
- British territory before 1763
- British gains after 1763
- Spanish territory

This map shows the amount of land lost by France and gained by Britain after the end of the war.

# THE COLONIES

By the middle of the 18th century, North America had been settled by colonists from many countries, including France, Spain, and Russia. It was the colonists from England, however, who eventually united to create a new nation. English settlers had established 13 colonies along the eastern coast of North America, from New England in the north to Georgia in the south.

**DID YOU KNOW?**
There were about 2.1 million colonists living in the 13 American colonies when the Revolutionary War started.

## The Southern Colonies

The Southern Colonies included Maryland, Virginia, North and South Carolina, and Georgia. Large estates produced corn, beef, pork, lumber, and rice. Farming paid well, but landowners needed people to work the fields and brought in slaves from across the Atlantic.

A family of southern landowners with one of their slaves.

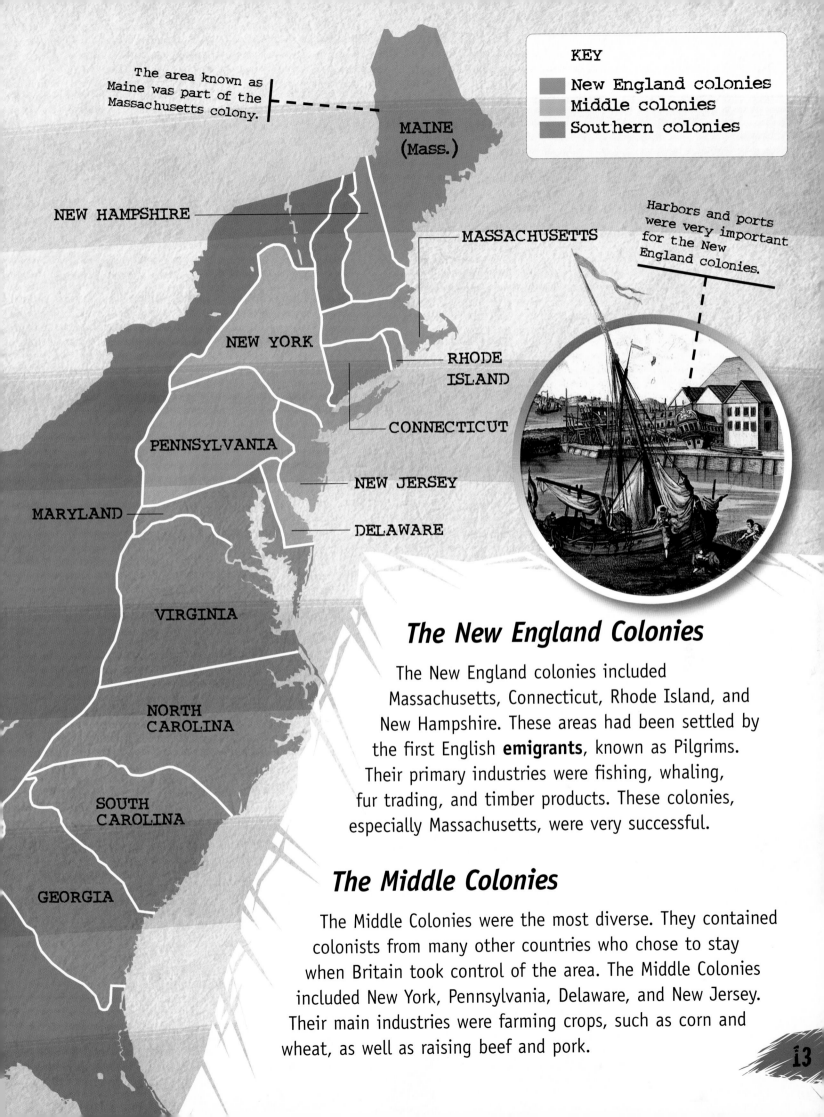

The area known as Maine was part of the Massachusetts colony.

MAINE (Mass.)

NEW HAMPSHIRE

MASSACHUSETTS

Harbors and ports were very important for the New England colonies.

NEW YORK

RHODE ISLAND

CONNECTICUT

PENNSYLVANIA

NEW JERSEY

MARYLAND

DELAWARE

VIRGINIA

NORTH CAROLINA

SOUTH CAROLINA

GEORGIA

## The New England Colonies

The New England colonies included Massachusetts, Connecticut, Rhode Island, and New Hampshire. These areas had been settled by the first English **emigrants**, known as Pilgrims. Their primary industries were fishing, whaling, fur trading, and timber products. These colonies, especially Massachusetts, were very successful.

## The Middle Colonies

The Middle Colonies were the most diverse. They contained colonists from many other countries who chose to stay when Britain took control of the area. The Middle Colonies included New York, Pennsylvania, Delaware, and New Jersey. Their main industries were farming crops, such as corn and wheat, as well as raising beef and pork.

# THE RULERS FROM FAR AWAY

On the other side of the Atlantic, Britain controlled one of the largest **empires** the world had ever seen. As well as colonies in North America, it controlled territories in Africa and Asia.

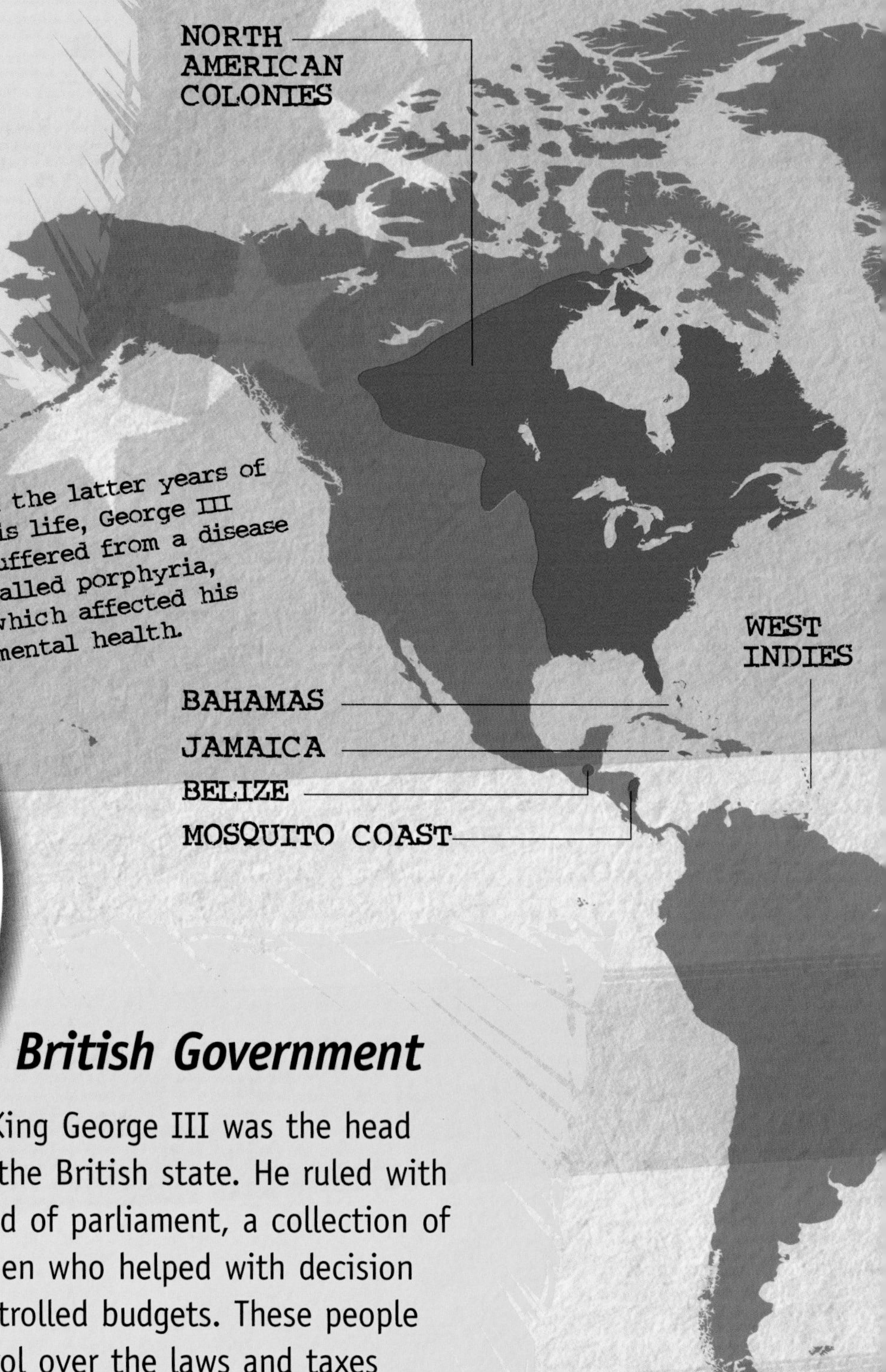

NORTH AMERICAN COLONIES

In the latter years of his life, George III suffered from a disease called porphyria, which affected his mental health.

WEST INDIES

BAHAMAS

JAMAICA

BELIZE

MOSQUITO COAST

## British Government

King George III was the head of the British state. He ruled with the aid of parliament, a collection of elected men who helped with decision making and controlled budgets. These people had ultimate control over the laws and taxes placed on people throughout the empire.

# The Seven Years' War

The French and Indian Wars formed part of a much larger conflict called the Seven Years' War (1756–1763). This involved every major power of the day, except for the Ottoman Empire. There were battles in Europe, Africa, and Asia, as well as in North America. At the end of the war, Britain and its allies, including Prussia, were victorious over a **coalition** that included Spain, France, and Austria.

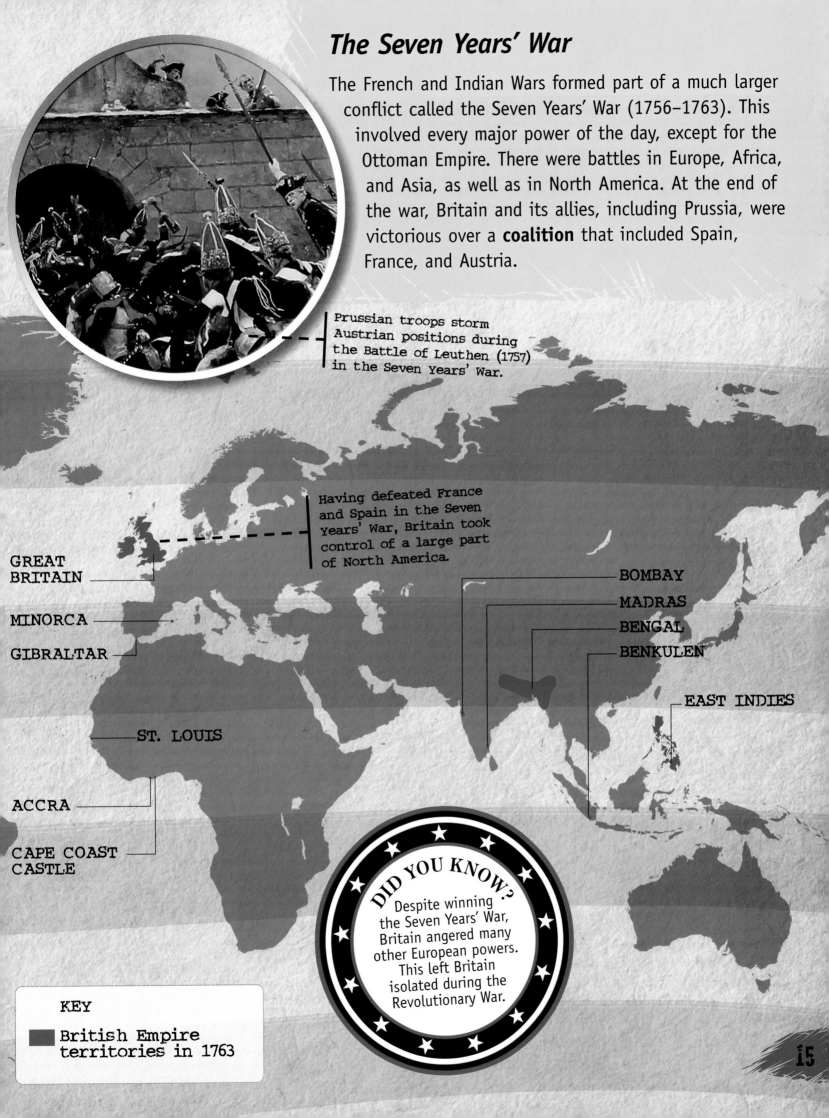

Prussian troops storm Austrian positions during the Battle of Leuthen (1757) in the Seven Years' War.

Having defeated France and Spain in the Seven Years' War, Britain took control of a large part of North America.

GREAT BRITAIN

MINORCA

GIBRALTAR

ST. LOUIS

ACCRA

CAPE COAST CASTLE

BOMBAY

MADRAS

BENGAL

BENKULEN

EAST INDIES

**DID YOU KNOW?**
Despite winning the Seven Years' War, Britain angered many other European powers. This left Britain isolated during the Revolutionary War.

**KEY**

British Empire territories in 1763

# TRIANGULAR TRADE

Britain established a network of trading links to make sure that money and goods flowed from its colonies and back to the ruling nation.

America to Europe

Africa to America

Cotton was grown throughout many of the southern states and was spun to make thread.

The three-sided trade routes were known as **"Triangular Trade."**

## America to Europe

After the slaves were taken off the ship, cotton, sugar, molasses, rum, and tobacco were loaded on board. The ships would then travel back to Britain to deliver the goods. Then the process would begin again. Sometimes, this round trip took a year to complete.

## Europe to Africa

Britain and other European countries sold bread, copper, cloth, and weapons to Africa.

Cloth was woven from the thread sent from the colonies.

## Manufactured Goods

Manufactured goods were also sent from Europe to trade in America. These included furniture, firearms, and cloth. Over time, the colonies began making the same goods as those made in Europe. It was an example of how the colonies were becoming more independent.

Europe to Africa

According to some sources, a total of 12.5 million slaves were shipped to the Americas.

Furniture made in Europe was shipped and sold to the colonies.

## Africa to America

When the goods reached West Africa, they were traded for slaves. The slaves were sent to the Caribbean and America to work on sugar, tobacco, and cotton **plantations**.

17

# THE STAMP ACT

British soldiers were kept in America to protect the colonies after the French and Indian War. They reminded colonists that they were still under British rule. However, soldiers were expensive and somebody needed to pay for them.

George Grenville was **Prime Minister** from 1763 to 1765.

## Creating the Tax

The British parliament was in charge of the treasury, controlling the money used by the government. In 1765, Prime Minister George Grenville created the Stamp Act. This came into effect on November 1, 1765, and forced colonists to pay extra for certain printed materials such as newspapers, playing cards, and legal documents.

**DID YOU KNOW?** Parliament had no idea the colonists would be upset about the Stamp Act. They thought colonists should help to pay for the soldiers.

Colonists wreck and burn property in protest at the Stamp Act.

## The Colonists Protest

Many colonists were furious, and not just because of the tax. Some believed their freedoms were being taken away. First, British soldiers were watching over them. Now, the British government created taxes that colonists were forced to pay. They believed they should have the right to vote about how they were taxed and what the taxes should pay for. Some colonists were so angry about the Stamp Act that they destroyed the property of local tax enforcers.

## End of the Act

Some colonists wrote a formal letter to the British government with their opinion. They wanted to have a say in how parliament developed and used taxes in the colonies. After much discussion in both Britain and the colonies, the Stamp Act was scrapped. After May 1, 1766, colonists no longer had to pay the tax.

This cartoon shows the Stamp Act being buried, with Grenville carrying its small coffin.

19

# SONS OF LIBERTY

As part of the protests against the Stamp Act, some colonists formed groups, calling themselves the "Sons of Liberty." They gathered in cities like Boston, New York, and Charleston, with the aim of uniting colonists against Britain.

The Sons of Liberty used a flag that had nine vertical red and white stripes.

## Who Were They?

The group took their name from a speech made by Irish politician Isaac Barré. Talking about the unfairness of the Stamp Act, Barré called the colonists "Sons of Liberty." Many people joined the groups. They were artisans, craftsmen, merchants, and farmers. They met secretly, because it was illegal to speak against the king of England. If discovered, they could've been hanged.

A group of Sons of Liberty supporters tar and feather a tax collector.

This Liberty Tree in Boston was one of many places where Patriots would meet and talk.

## What Did They Do?

The Sons of Liberty wrote letters and pamphlets explaining why British rule was wrong. They also carried out violent acts, burning offices that belonged to British leaders, and even **tarring and feathering** people who were loyal to the king. They pinned notes to trees, which became known as "Liberty Trees." As more men joined the Sons of Liberty, more Liberty Trees were designated as meeting places.

**DID YOU KNOW?**

During the Revolutionary War, Loyalist forces cut down the Liberty Tree in Boston and used it as fuel. This only angered the Patriots even more.

# MORE TAXES, MORE ANGER

The British still needed to raise money, so they introduced more taxes on the colonists. Again, some colonists were upset that they had no say in the taxes and laws that the British parliament forced on them.

## The Townshend Acts

Starting on March 24, 1765, the British military commander in America, General Thomas Gage, demanded that colonists house and feed the troops. In June 1767, Charles Townshend introduced taxes on glass, lead, paint, and tea to pay for the soldiers. The colonists were only allowed to get these items from England.

Charles Townshend was British **Chancellor of the Exchequer** at the time.

This engraving by Paul Revere shows British troops arriving at Boston in 1768.

John Dickinson was one of the richest men in the colonies.

## Colonist Reaction

John Dickinson was a solicitor and politician from Philadelphia. He suggested **boycotting** British goods. The colonists refused to buy goods coming from Britain. There were also protests and riots in Boston, and British soldiers were sent there in 1768 to try to stop the violence. The boycott and protests worked, however, and on April 12, 1770, the Townshend Acts ended.

23

# THE BOSTON MASSACRE

The colonists were not happy about the presence of British troops. Some treated the soldiers poorly by teasing and throwing rocks at them. This behavior, however, would have terrible consequences.

## A Soldier's Fear

On the night of March 5, 1770, a group of colonists in Boston surrounded a British guard and began shouting at him. The guard loaded his **musket** and called for help. British Captain Thomas Preston led a small group of soldiers to help the guard and break apart the mob, which was growing angry. Suddenly, a shot rang out and more firing followed. Five colonists were killed. Preston left with his soldiers before anyone else was hurt.

The massacre took place outside the Old State House, which still stands today.

Paul Revere's etching of the massacre shows British soldiers firing on unarmed colonists.

## Two Sides to the Story

Some people believed the soldiers fired first, while others thought they acted in self-defense. Even so, the British soldiers were tried for murder. Only two of them were found guilty, but they were soon released. Many colonists were angry about this and used the killings as **propaganda**. They started to spread the message that the British were dangerous and not to be trusted.

**DID YOU KNOW?**
Crispus Attucks was one of the first men killed for the Patriot cause in the Boston Massacre. He became a symbol for African-American heroism.

# BOSTON TEA PARTY

In May 1773, the British government passed the Tea Act, which forced colonists to buy tea from Britain. This angered the colonists, who still wanted representation in the British parliament.

Thomas Hutchinson was the **Governor** of Boston until 1774. He did not think Patriot leaders would destroy so much property. He was wrong.

**DID YOU KNOW?** Some colonists believed the tea merchants should be paid for the tea—they weren't responsible for the laws.

## Dress Up

On December 16, 1773, three ships carrying tea from Britain sat in Boston Harbor. Colonists, possibly led by Samuel Adams, refused to let the tea be unloaded—they did not want to buy the tea and pay taxes to Britain. The Sons of Liberty took action. Some dressed up as Mohawk tribesmen and boarded the ships, dumping 340 chests of tea into the harbor.

This replica of one of the tea ships is in Boston Harbor today.

## The Result

The British parliament was furious. The tea was extremely valuable and they expected to be repaid. Parliament closed the port of Boston until they got their money back, which meant colonists could not receive or send goods and services. People on both sides were angry.

The colonists didn't damage the boats. They wanted their message to be clear: They would not buy anything that supported Britain.

# COERCIVE ACTS

The Boston Tea Party cost the British parliament in lost taxes and also undermined its authority. In the first months of 1774, parliament introduced the Coercive Acts to teach the people of Boston a lesson.

**DID YOU KNOW?**
The Patriots called the Coercive Acts the "Intolerable Acts" because they were so punishing and the colonists had not been asked about them.

Ships came to Boston to bring supplies the colonists needed.

## Closing the Port

The Coercive Acts closed the port of Boston. Only food, fuel, and British military supplies were allowed to enter the town. This hurt the people of Boston, who depended on shipping to sell and receive goods. With the port closed, Boston colonists lost money and ran low on supplies.

## No Trials in Massachusetts

Sometimes fights would break out between British soldiers and colonists. When this happened, a trial usually followed, but the trials no longer took place in Boston. Many colonists felt that misbehaving British soldiers would not get punished. In response to these new laws, all the colonies united. They started to send supplies to Boston and they began talking to one another about what they should do.

## A New Governor

General Thomas Gage was made governor of Massachusetts to enforce the new laws. Colonists were no longer allowed to meet without the governor being present. He also appointed new officers, which took even more power away from the colonists. It meant that they could no longer have a say in what happened in their own colonies.

Thomas Gage was the Governor of Massachusetts from 1774 to 1775.

29

# CONTINENTAL CONGRESS

Colonial leaders decided that they needed to organize their own body to negotiate with the British and to govern themselves. They formed the **Continental Congress** and it met three times from 1774 to 1789.

The First Continental Congress met at Carpenter's Hall in Philadelphia, Pennsylvania.

Samuel Adams was a delegate for Massachusetts at the Continental Congress.

## First Decisions

Some delegates thought bigger colonies should have more power when it was time to vote and make decisions. Others believed each colony was equal, and they should all have equal votes. After discussion, everybody agreed all the colonies were equal and they should each have the same votes.

**DID YOU KNOW?**
The first five Presidents of the United States served in the Continental Congress: Washington, Adams, Jefferson, Madison, and Monroe.

## Standing Against Britain

Congress wrote a list of problems they had with British leaders. It was called the "Declaration and Resolves." Colonists believed they were "entitled to life, liberty, and property" in America. Only when they had these would they buy or sell goods with Britain.

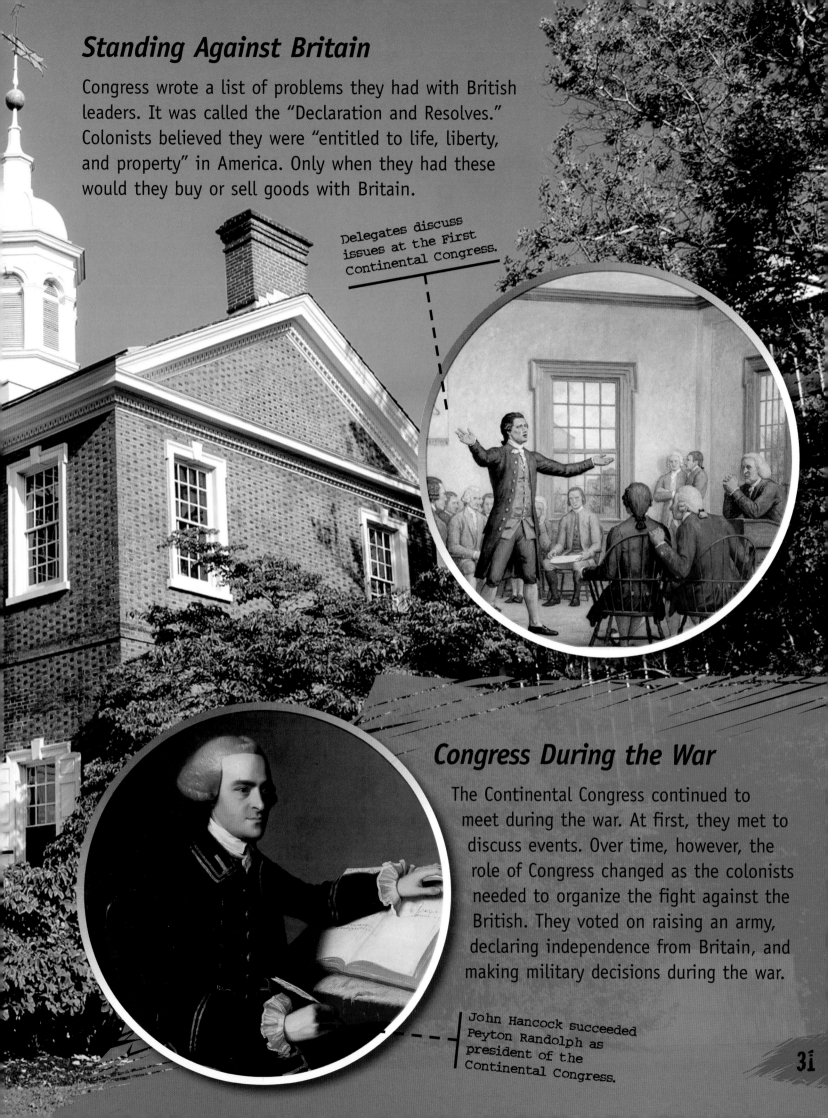

Delegates discuss issues at the First Continental Congress.

## Congress During the War

The Continental Congress continued to meet during the war. At first, they met to discuss events. Over time, however, the role of Congress changed as the colonists needed to organize the fight against the British. They voted on raising an army, declaring independence from Britain, and making military decisions during the war.

John Hancock succeeded Peyton Randolph as president of the Continental Congress.

33

# PAUL REVERE'S MIDNIGHT RIDE

The Patriots wanted to protect themselves in case British soldiers began to attack. They began storing weapons throughout the colonies. British spies learned that Patriots were storing cannons and weapons in Concord, Massachusetts. Thomas Gage, the commander of the British army, needed to destroy them. General Gage also had orders to arrest Patriot leaders John Hancock and Samuel Adams for speaking out against the king.

## One if by Land, Two if by Sea

Colonists had their own spies. They knew General Gage was planning to send troops to Concord. They needed to warn the Patriots that British soldiers were coming. Paul Revere told colonists to hang out one lantern if the soldiers were coming to Concord by land, and hang out two lanterns if they were coming across the Charles River.

**DID YOU KNOW?**

Before the war, Revere was an engraver and silversmith. After the war, he went back to metalworking, making cannons and armor for ships.

# Paul Revere and His Ride

On April 18, 1775, Paul Revere left at 11:00 p.m. to warn Hancock and Adams that British officers were on their way. Then he and two other Patriots, William Dawes and Dr. Samuel Prescott, hurried to warn those living in Lexington and Concord that British soldiers were coming to destroy the weapons they were hiding.

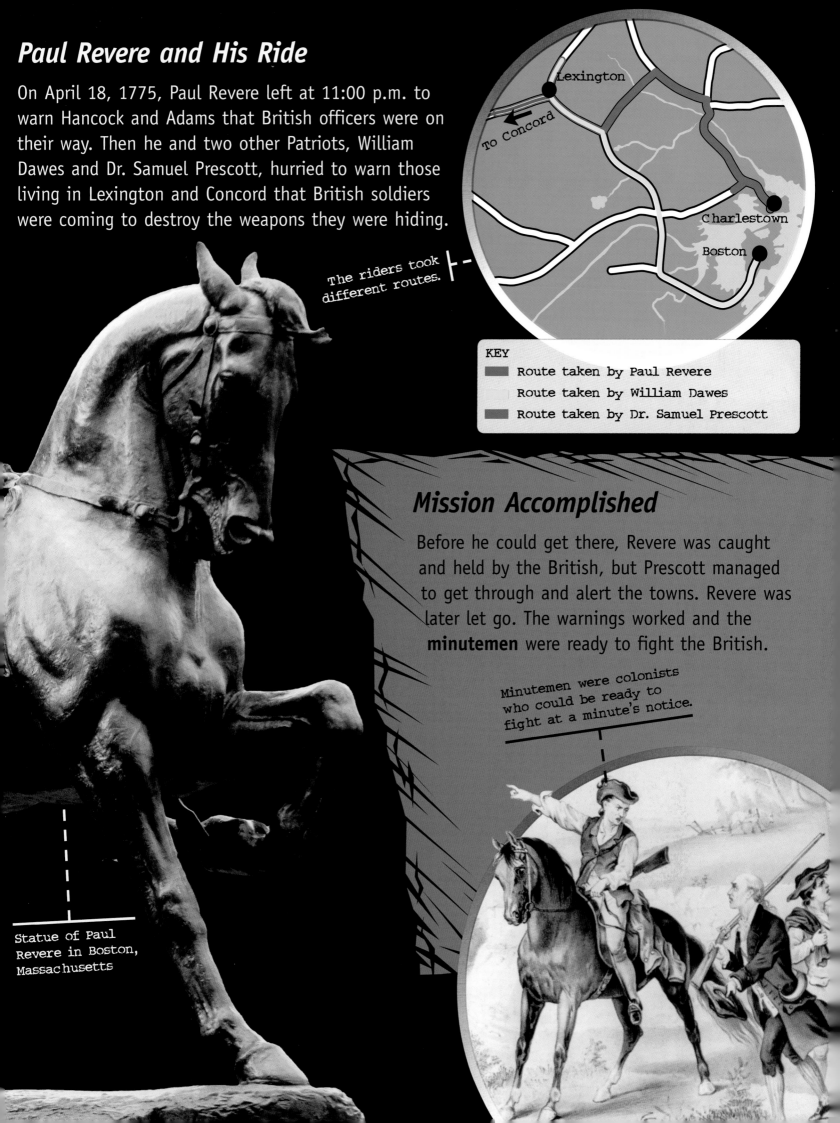

The riders took different routes.

Lexington

To Concord

Charlestown

Boston

**KEY**
Route taken by Paul Revere
Route taken by William Dawes
Route taken by Dr. Samuel Prescott

## Mission Accomplished

Before he could get there, Revere was caught and held by the British, but Prescott managed to get through and alert the towns. Revere was later let go. The warnings worked and the **minutemen** were ready to fight the British.

Minutemen were colonists who could be ready to fight at a minute's notice.

Statue of Paul Revere in Boston, Massachusetts

# THE BATTLE OF LEXINGTON AND CONCORD

British troops marched out of Boston in April 1775 to capture and destroy storages of weapons in Concord belonging to the colonists. However, they didn't realize that the colonists were waiting for them and were prepared to make a stand in what marked the start of the Revolutionary War.

The British had to march through Lexington before reaching Concord.

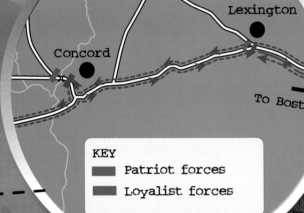

**KEY**
- Patriot forces
- Loyalist forces

## BATTLE BRIEF

- **Date:** April 18–19, 1775
- **Patriot Leader:** Captain John Parker
- **Loyalist Leader:** General Thomas Gage
- **Objective:** The British wanted to capture Patriot leaders Sam Adams and John Hancock and seize colonial weapons
- **Victory:** The Patriots

## An Unexpected Fight

General Gage hoped his men could reach Concord quickly. By the time they got to Lexington, a force of colonial Minutemen was already there. General Gage ordered the colonists to put down their weapons. Someone fired a shot, but nobody knows who it was. A British officer ordered his soldiers to open fire. Most of the Patriots fled, and the British soldiers moved on.

## On to Concord

The British had no idea that about 3,500 colonists were waiting at Concord. When the two forces met, muskets began to fire. This time the colonists were ready and they fired back, holding their ground. The British soldiers were forced to retreat back toward Boston.

British troops open fire on militiamen at Lexington.

**DID YOU KNOW?**

Ralph Waldo Emerson wrote a poem called "Concord Hymn" in which he describes the first shot of the war as the "shot heard round the world."

## The Result

The British weren't able to confiscate the colonists' weapons and it was now clear to both sides that war was inevitable. The British realized they would need more troops to fight the colonists. The colonists realized they could stand up to one of the most powerful armies in the world.

# UNIFORMS

Uniforms helped to identify one group of soldiers from another and they helped distinguish officers from their soldiers. They were also designed to be seen on the smoke and confusion of the battlefield.

**DID YOU KNOW?**
Washington knew uniforms were important to build morale. Throughout the war he wrote to Congress about the need for more uniforms.

Some Patriots still wore coats from the French and Indian War.

British soldiers were called "Lobsterbacks" or "Redcoats" because of their red uniforms.

## British Soldiers

British soldiers wore scarlet, which made them easy to spot on a smoky battlefield. Each soldier was only given one set of clothing. A waistcoat, linen shirt, breeches, stockings, and leather shoes were also provided.

## American Uniforms

At the start of the war, the Patriots were not organized as an official army and they did not have matching uniforms. Men fought in the clothes they owned or whatever they could find. Green and brown coats were the most popular, because fabric was available in those colors. Between 1777 and 1778, Congress ordered 40,000 uniforms for the expanding army. Throughout the war, however, regular supplies were hard to find and shortages of clothing and equipment were common.

## Properly Equipped

Besides his weapons, a properly equipped soldier would have a leather pouch or tin box holding ammunition, a musket tool, and a supply of flint used to fire the musket. He would carry a haversack to carry food, utensils, and a cup. A knapsack would hold extra clothing or personal items if the soldier had any.

Musketmen had to carry all the equipment needed to fire and maintain their weapons during a battle.

37

# WEAPONS

British soldiers were given weapons because they were part of an organized army. American colonists, however, had to use their own weapons, if they even had any. As the war went on, George Washington did his best to make sure each soldier in his army had a weapon.

**DID YOU KNOW?**
Muskets fired a one-ounce lead ball. The muskets were loaded by ramming the ball, gunpowder, and wadding in through the muzzle.

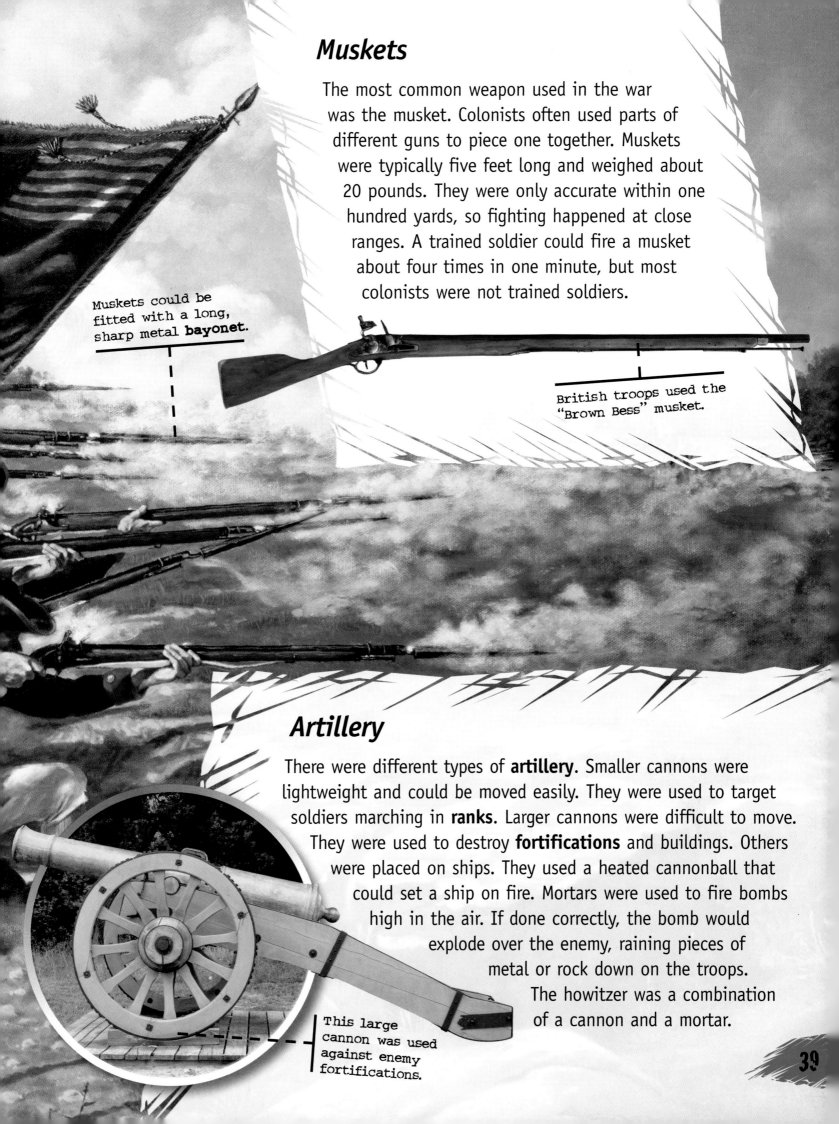

## Muskets

The most common weapon used in the war was the musket. Colonists often used parts of different guns to piece one together. Muskets were typically five feet long and weighed about 20 pounds. They were only accurate within one hundred yards, so fighting happened at close ranges. A trained soldier could fire a musket about four times in one minute, but most colonists were not trained soldiers.

Muskets could be fitted with a long, sharp metal **bayonet**.

British troops used the "Brown Bess" musket.

## Artillery

There were different types of **artillery**. Smaller cannons were lightweight and could be moved easily. They were used to target soldiers marching in **ranks**. Larger cannons were difficult to move. They were used to destroy **fortifications** and buildings. Others were placed on ships. They used a heated cannonball that could set a ship on fire. Mortars were used to fire bombs high in the air. If done correctly, the bomb would explode over the enemy, raining pieces of metal or rock down on the troops. The howitzer was a combination of a cannon and a mortar.

This large cannon was used against enemy fortifications.

# FORT TICONDEROGA

Fort Ticonderoga was built in 1755 and used in the French and Indian War. It was located on Lake Champlain in northeastern New York. This was an important position where armies could access Canada and the Hudson River Valley. British troops had occupied the fort since the end of the French and Indian War.

## BATTLE BRIEF

- **Date:** May 10, 1775
- **Patriot Leaders:** Ethan Allen and Captain Benedict Arnold
- **Loyalist Leader:** Captain William de la Place
- **Objective:** The Patriots wanted to capture the fort and the weapons held there
- **Victory:** The Patriots

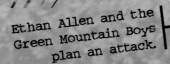

Ethan Allen and the Green Mountain Boys plan an attack.

## Sneak Attack

The Patriots wanted to steal cannons and other weapons stored at the fort. Ethan Allen, commander of the Green Mountain Boys, and Captain Benedict Arnold, both Patriot leaders, organized a group of men to seize Fort Ticonderoga. On May 10, 1775, they packed 85 men into boats and moved up the river during a horrible storm. The storm covered any noise they made as they approached the fort.

# Ethan Allen Demands Surrender

The surprise attack worked. Allen and Arnold charged at the fort with their men. The Patriots caught the British soldiers while they were unarmed and sleeping. Allen demanded that the British commander, Captain de la Place, surrender the fort. The captain saw his men were already surrendering and decided to give up.

British soldiers were caught by surprise by the daring Patriot raid.

Fort Ticonderoga stood at a key access point to Canada and the Hudson River Valley.

## The Prize

The Patriots seized 78 working cannons, mortars, and howitzers, as well as cannonballs, flint, and gunpowder. They also took the men, women, and children staying at the fort prisoner.

**DID YOU KNOW?**
The name Ticonderoga comes from the Iroquois word meaning "it is at the junction of two waterways."

43

# GEORGE WASHINGTON

The Patriots needed a proven military leader to command their new army. They turned to George Washington, who had fought in the French and Indian War.

Washington (on the white horse) showed great bravery at the Battle of Monongahela on July 9, 1755, during the French and Indian War.

## Early Life

George was born in 1732. He was a hard worker and very smart. He first joined the military in 1753. One of his first battles, during the French and Indian War, ended in defeat and embarrassment. Washington learned from his mistakes and was determined to be an excellent leader.

Washington was born in this house in Westmoreland County, Virginia.

## Elected Leader

On June 15, 1775, the Continental Congress elected Washington to be the leader of the new **Continental Army.** Washington worked hard to keep Congress informed about events on the battlefield. He also stayed in contact with military units throughout the country.

Washington accepts command of the Continental Army.

**DID YOU KNOW?**
When he was 14 years old, George Washington tried to join the British **Royal Navy,** but his mother wouldn't let him.

## Duties

As the military leader, Washington needed to know how many soldiers were fighting in the war. It was his job to make sure they were dressed, fed, and had shelter. He also needed to know where the British soldiers were and which Patriot soldiers were available to fight them when necessary.

When Washington attended meetings of the Continental Congress, he was the only member who dressed in military uniform.

43

# RAISING AN ARMY

Both sides contained soldiers from different backgrounds. They were organized into many different types of fighting units.

Soldiers of the Continental Army

## Militias

Each of the 13 colonies had its own **militia**. These were made up of men old enough to serve and who received basic training from an experienced military leader. They would live at home, but would leave their families and fight as a unit, sometimes at a moment's notice.

44

## Regulars and the Continental Army

Long-serving regulars were under direction from their state leaders. Militias and regulars could fight in battles, but more often they were used to annoy the enemy. They hid behind trees and fired at Loyalists as they moved about. The soldiers in the Continental Army served under the commander, George Washington. These men usually fought in large-scale battles.

About 30,000 Hessian troops fought in the Revolutionary War.

## Hessians and Redcoats

**Hessian** soldiers came from the German state of Hesse-Kassel. Several countries, including Savoy, Sweden, and Britain, hired these troops to fight their wars for them. The British soldiers were some of the best-trained troops in the world at the time. They were career troops. Many started in the army when they turned 17, and served as soldiers until they were no longer able to fight.

# BATTLE OF BUNKER HILL

After the Battle of Lexington and Concord, the British retreated and took control of Boston. The Patriots wanted to drive the British out of Boston and on the night of June 16, 1775, they quickly built fortifications on two hills, Breed's Hill and Bunker Hill, that both overlooked the city and harbor. The British were taken by surprise and had no choice but to try and drive the Patriots from their positions.

British soldiers marched up Breed's Hill in ranks to attack Patriot positions.

## The British Attack

The fortifications were strong and British artillery did little damage. British soldiers arrived by boat. As they marched up Breed's Hill, the Patriots fired down on them, killing them easily. Surviving British troops withdrew, reorganized, and charged. Again, they were killed easily, and the surviving soldiers retreated down the hill.

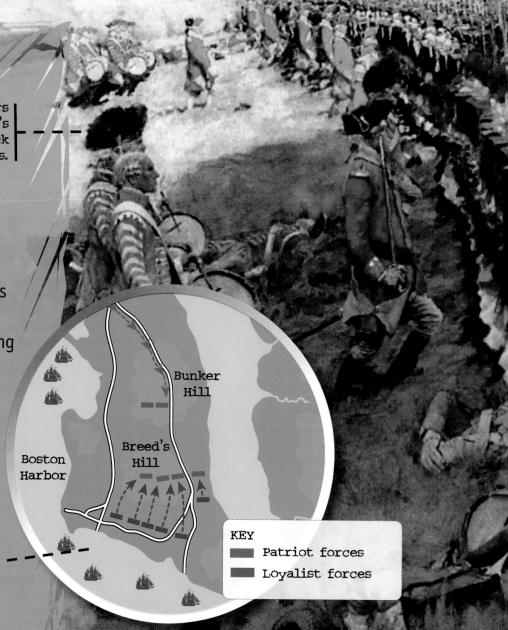

Bunker Hill

Breed's Hill

Boston Harbor

KEY
Patriot forces
Loyalist forces

Although known as the Battle of Bunker Hill, most of the action took place on Breed's Hill

# BATTLE BRIEF

- ⚜ **Date:** June 16–17, 1775
- ⚜ **Patriot Leaders:**
  Colonel William Prescott, Major General Israel Putnam
- ⚜ **Loyalist Leaders:**
  Major General William Howe, General Henry Clinton
- ⚜ **Objective:** Patriots could fire on British ships in Boston Harbor, as well as the British soldiers inside Boston
- ⚜ **Victory:** The Loyalists

The Patriot commander General Warren was killed during the British attack.

**DID YOU KNOW?**
The Patriots had little gunpowder compared to the British. They were ordered not to fire "until you see the whites of their eyes."

## A Costly Victory

The Patriots were running out of ammunition and started throwing rocks. When the British came up the hill a third time, both sides fought with bayonets and muskets. The British overran the forts, and the Patriots were forced to withdraw. The British won the battle, but lost almost half of their soldiers. They learned that the war would be hard, while the Patriots realized that they could take on the British.

# USING THE LAND

During a battle, the shape of the land can often be very helpful, but it can also make things even harder. Military leaders have learned how to use physical features in military strategy to their advantage.

At the top of Breed's Hill, British troops still had to scale the Patriot fortifications.

## Fields and Hills

It's easier to fire down onto an enemy from a high position and it's harder to attack up a hill to take that position. As such, defenders try to establish themselves on high ground, ideally surrounded by open countryside. At the Battle of Bunker Hill, Patriots fortified two hilltops and British troops were forced to march up the open hillsides. Patriot musketmen were able to kill many British soldiers before they could reach the American positions.

## Harbors

Navigating harbors can be difficult. In Charleston Harbor, South Carolina, the British navy was unaware of the sandbars and shoals. In their attempt to attack a fort in Charleston, many British ships got stuck, making them perfect targets for the Patriots to fire upon.

Charleston Harbor contains many natural obstacles.

## Rivers

Transporting soldiers by boat can be faster and sometimes easier than having them march. It can also be quieter, so soldiers can sneak up on the enemy. Both Patriot and Loyalist troops traveled by water whenever possible.

Forts were often built near rivers.

# BATTLE OF MACHIAS

The Battle of Machias was one of the first naval battles of the American Revolution. It took place around the port of Machias in what is now the state of Maine.

## BATTLE BRIEF

☀ **Date:** June 11–12, 1775

☀ **Patriot Leader:**
Jeremiah O'Brien

☀ **Loyalist Leader:**
James Moore

☀ **Objective:** To stop British soldiers from receiving supplies

☀ **Victory:** The Patriots

The *Margaretta* was a **schooner**, like this modern replica.

## The Background

By the middle of 1775, British troops were trapped in Boston and surrounded by angry colonists. They needed supplies to strengthen their army. One businessman, Ichabod Jones, wanted to help the British and their commander James Moore. He offered to provide the soldiers much-needed supplies. When the colonists found out, they were angry. They decided to capture Jones and then try to capture Moore. When Moore heard of this plan, he escaped on his schooner *Margaretta*.

## The Chase

Patriot leader Jeremiah O'Brien gathered a crew and boarded another ship, *Unity*. It chased and caught the *Margaretta*. James Moore ordered his men to fire the cannons, but the cannonballs simply fell into the ocean. Muskets were fired from both ships and James Moore was shot. Soon after, the Patriots boarded and captured the *Margaretta*. Moore died two days later.

The *Margaretta* opens fire on the chasing *Unity*.

## The Result

Jeremiah O'Brien went on to organize a small **fleet** of ships. They captured British merchant ships that were trying to take supplies to the British in Boston.

# NAVAL FORCES

The British had one of the most powerful navies in the world, while the colonists had no navy at all. When France joined the Americans, their powerful navy helped the Patriots to win the war.

## Ruling the Waves

At the start of the war, the British Royal Navy had a fleet of nearly 500 warships. They were equipped with cannons and could attack Patriot forts along the coast. The British navy also had more than 7,000 cargo ships which they used to bring supplies and more troops.

The British fleet was commanded by Admiral Richard Howe.

## Gathering a Navy

The Americans had no warships with cannons or guns. Private boat owners with whaling boats or schooners did their best to damage British ships and steal supplies. They were even successful in stealing British warships. In October 1775, the Continental Congress formally ordered the creation of the **Continental Navy** and the construction of their own warships.

John Paul Jones was a hero of the Continental Navy.

## France to the Rescue

When France joined the American cause in 1778, the French navy was a great help. They often battled British ships before they could cross the Atlantic. This made it difficult for Britain to get much-needed supplies to North America.

An American warship defeats and captures a British ship.

# THE BATTLE OF QUEBEC

After the French and Indian War, Canada fell under British control. The Patriots wanted to capture Quebec and try to convince the Canadians to join their fight against Britain.

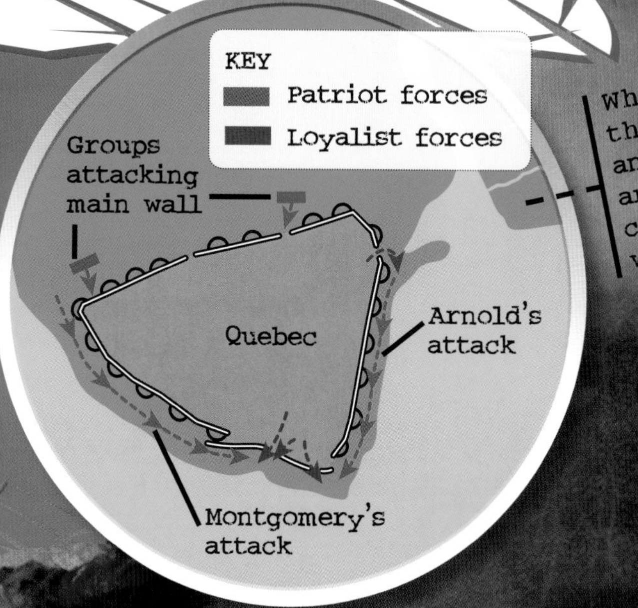

**KEY**
- Patriot forces
- Loyalist forces

Groups attacking main wall

Quebec

Arnold's attack

Montgomery's attack

While two groups attacked the main wall, Montgomery and Arnold led two forces around either side of the city. However, both groups were beaten back.

**DID YOU KNOW?**
Montgomery was a British officer before the Revolutionary War. However, he agreed with the views of the Patriots and sided with them.

## Plans and Problems

Benedict Arnold led about 1,200 men along the Kennebec River through Maine. At the same time, Patriot General Richard Montgomery brought 3,000 men towards Montreal. The two armies would meet at Quebec and fight the Loyalists. There were problems from the beginning. The cold northern winter made traveling nearly impossible and there was little food. Many soldiers fell ill or left and went home.

Only 600 of Arnold's original force arrived at Quebec to launch the attack.

General Montgomery is killed during the attack on Quebec.

## The Battle

Arnold and Montgomery joined forces outside Quebec. The remaining Patriot soldiers were cold, starving, and sick. Inside Quebec, the Loyalist soldiers were rested and ready. When the Patriots attempted a surprise attack during a snow storm on December 31, the Loyalists were ready. Nearly 500 Patriots were killed, injured, or taken prisoner. Less than 20 Loyalists were hurt. The Battle of Quebec was a disaster.

## BATTLE BRIEF

- **Date:** December 31, 1775
- **Patriot Leaders:** Major Benedict Arnold, General Richard Montgomery
- **Loyalist Leaders:** Guy Carleton, General Allen Maclean
- **Objective:** To turn Canadians against Britain
- **Victory:** The Loyalists

# BETSY ROSS AND THE AMERICAN FLAG

Americans still used many of the flags and symbols from the British Empire. But they were determined to create symbols and an identity of their own.

**DID YOU KNOW?**
According to tradition, the new flag was first raised by the Continental Army in June 1777 during its seasonal camp at Middlebrook, New Jersey.

The Grand Union Flag

## Many Different Flags

When colonists first settled North America, they were loyal to Britain and they identified with the British flag. As tension with Britain increased, many colonists and militia groups created their own flags. When George Washington took control of the Continental Army on January 1, 1776, he ordered the Grand Union Flag raised to unite the colonies. This featured 13 red and white stripes with the Union Jack in the top left corner.

## A New Flag

While no one is certain who designed and made the first American flag to feature the stars and stripes, the most popular story concerns Elizabeth "Betsy" Ross. According to legend, she was approached in Spring 1776 by a party from the Continental Congress, including George Washington, to make a new flag for the Patriots.

The first 13 stars were arranged in a circle against a blue background.

## Adopting the New Flag

Betsy is said to have made several changes to the design suggested by Congress, including using stars with five points, rather than six. On June 14, 1777, Congress passed the Flag Act, making the flag official. The act stated: "that the flag of the United States be made of thirteen stripes, alternate red and white; that the union be thirteen stars, white in a blue field, representing a new Constellation."

# WRITING THE DECLARATION OF INDEPENDENCE

By the spring of 1776, many states were speaking of independence and of breaking completely from British rule. If the colonies became independent, they also had to decide what kind of country they would be.

**DID YOU KNOW?**
New York was the only colony not to vote for independence during the second vote. Its representatives had not been given permission to do so.

## Debating What to Do

On June 7, 1776, the Continental Congress met at the Pennsylvania State House in Philadelphia. The delegates debated and decided to speak with the people in their home states. Thomas Jefferson, a member of the Continental Congress and a well-known writer, began drafting a statement of declaration. Benjamin Franklin, John Adams, Roger Sherman, and Robert R. Livingston helped.

Franklin, Adams, and Jefferson writing the Declaration.

## The Vote

On July 1, delegates voted to determine if they would declare independence or not. Nine colonies voted in favor, two colonies voted against, and two were undecided. The delegates hoped the decision would be unanimous. They talked even more and voted again on July 2. This time, 12 colonies voted for independence, so it was decided—the colonies were officially breaking free from Britain.

The room where the Declaration was adopted by Congress.

After the second vote, Congress spent the next few days editing the draft of the Declaration.

## A New Nation

Thomas Jefferson, Benjamin Franklin, John Adams, and others worked hard to get the words just right. Once the language was agreed, the Declaration was printed on the night of July 4. The purpose of the Declaration of Independence was to firmly state that America was no longer under British rule. It let other countries around the world know that they could befriend the American nation and fight with them against Britain.

# SIGNING THE DECLARATION

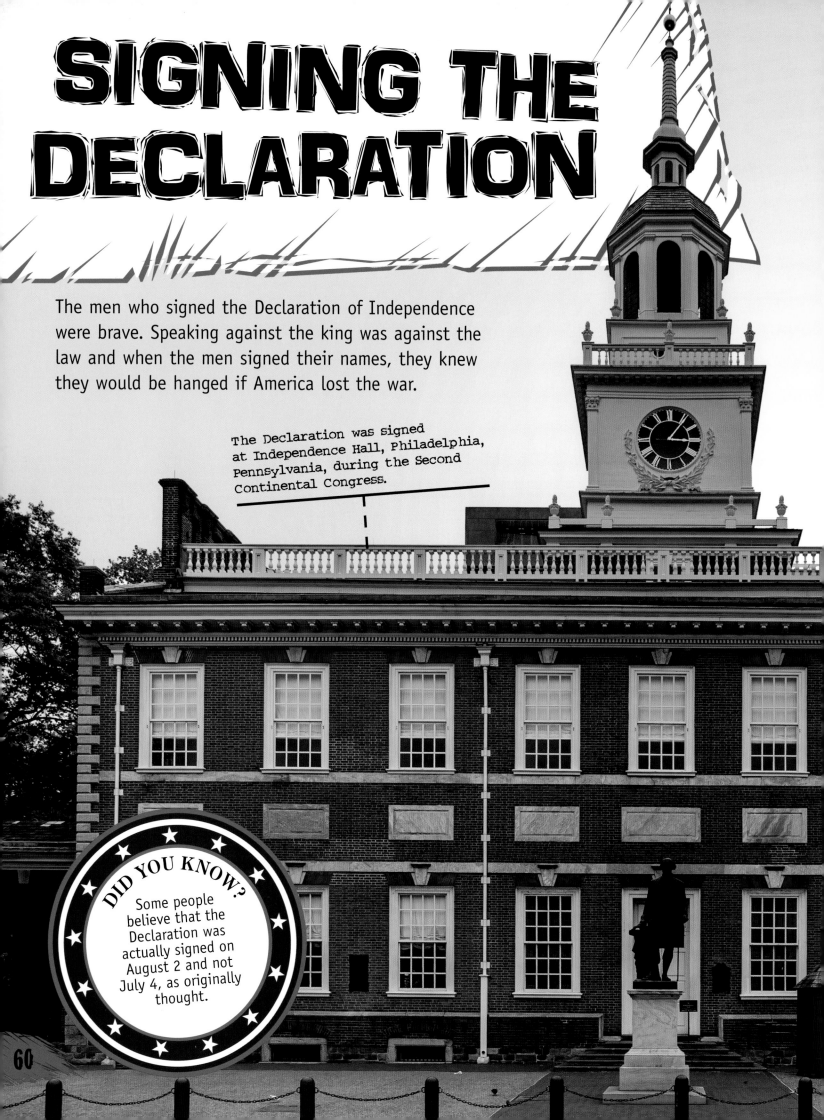

The men who signed the Declaration of Independence were brave. Speaking against the king was against the law and when the men signed their names, they knew they would be hanged if America lost the war.

The Declaration was signed at Independence Hall, Philadelphia, Pennsylvania, during the Second Continental Congress.

**DID YOU KNOW?**
Some people believe that the Declaration was actually signed on August 2 and not July 4, as originally thought.

The Declaration has the signatures of 56 congressional delegates, with John Hancock's signature being the largest.

## Signing the Declaration

The first to sign was John Hancock, who was president of Congress at the time. Then the delegates signed in columns across the document. They signed by state from north to south. Eight days later, George III and the British parliament learned the news.

## Spreading the News

In the days following the completion of the document, bells rang out to summon people to hear the document being read. Copies of the document were taken to the army and state legislatures to let everyone know that the colonies were a new nation: the United States of America.

The Liberty Bell was rung in Philadelphia so that people could hear the Declaration being read.

# THE FALL OF NEW YORK

## BATTLE BRIEF

- ✵ **Date:** August 1776
- ✵ **Patriot Leaders:** George Washington, Major General Israel Putnam
- ✵ **Loyalist Leader:** General William Howe
- ✵ **Objective:** The British wanted to seize New York City and isolate the New England colonies from the rest
- ✵ **Victory:** The Loyalists captured New York City, though the Patriots managed to win a smaller battle in Manhattan

British ships began arriving at New York City in June, 1776. By the end of July, there were more than 24,000 British soldiers ready to fight. The British also surrounded New York City with their ships. On August 22, British soldiers landed on Long Island.

**KEY**

▬ Patriot forces
▬ Loyalist forces

New York City

Long Island

The Patriots escaped before they were surrounded.

## The Battle

British soldiers quickly surrounded the Patriots, and it looked like Washington and almost 20,000 soldiers would be captured. Luckily, a storm rolled in and the conditions made things difficult for the British, giving Washington and his army time to escape.

## The Rescue

Washington needed to get his men out of Long Island quickly. A group of 500 Patriots led by Colonel Glover were close and they also happened to be fishermen. They quietly moved the Patriot soldiers from Long Island to safety. The Americans lost about 1,000 men. They retreated to Manhattan Island to face the British again.

Patriot troops load a cannon during the retreat from Long Island.

British ships unload troops in the run-up to the fall of New York.

**DID YOU KNOW?**
The Patriots tried blocking the Hudson, Harlem, and East Rivers with debris, making it harder for British ships to navigate them.

## Hope for the Patriots

Washington refused to give up. He decided to defend Harlem Heights, located at the north end of Manhattan. The Patriots attacked a smaller group of British soldiers there. The fight was short, but the Patriots were victorious. It was enough to help the colonists gain confidence after losing New York City.

# THE BATTLE OF TRENTON

The British hired about 30,000 Hessian troops from Germany to help them fight the Patriots. They were stationed in Trenton, New Jersey. George Washington knew Christmas Day was an important day for the Hessians. They would be eating, drinking, and relaxing. He used this information to his advantage.

**KEY**
■ Patriot forces
■ Loyalist forces

Delaware River

Trenton

The Americans crossed the Delaware to surprise the Hessians.

## BATTLE BRIEF

☀ **Date:** December 25–26, 1776

☀ **Patriot Leaders:** George Washington, Major General Nathanael Greene

☀ **Loyalist Leader:** Colonel Johann Rall (Hessian troops)

☀ **Objective:** The Patriots needed to secure New Jersey and they also needed to capture British supplies

☀ **Victory:** The Patriots

## Crossing the Delaware

A horrible winter storm was raging. Washington gathered 2,500 American soldiers. To capture the town, the Continental Army had to cross the Delaware River. It was 800 feet of floating ice with a strong current. Wind and hail whipped at the men, but every soldier, horse, and weapon made it across. They began marching toward Trenton.

## The Attack

The Hessians were not expecting an attack and weren't prepared. Washington's men surprised them. They did not have time to organize themselves and fight back and the battle lasted just 40 minutes. The survivors surrendered, and the Continental Army captured 918 Hessian soldiers. The battle gave the Patriots confidence to keep fighting.

**DID YOU KNOW?**
The Hessian troops made up about one-quarter of all the soldiers the British sent to fight in the war.

This painting shows Washington and his troops crossing the Delaware River.

Washington receives the surrender of the Hessian commander.

# THE BATTLE OF PRINCETON

## KEY

▬ Patriot forces
▬ Loyalist forces

Princeton

Trenton

Washington succeeded in surprising the British troops.

Washington knew the British would come back to claim Trenton, so he decided to attack again. He took 2,000 of his men toward Princeton. However, Charles Cornwallis, a British general, had 8,000 men.

## DID YOU KNOW?

Washington's success was partly because of a brave spy named Colonel John Cadwalader. He created a detailed map of British positions.

## The Battle

On January 2, the two forces met at Assunpink Creek. Both sides were exhausted and began to retreat. Cornwallis believed he had the Patriots trapped and took his soldiers back to their camp. Washington saw his chance. His soldiers built campfires to trick the British into thinking they were making camp for the night. General Washington had other plans.

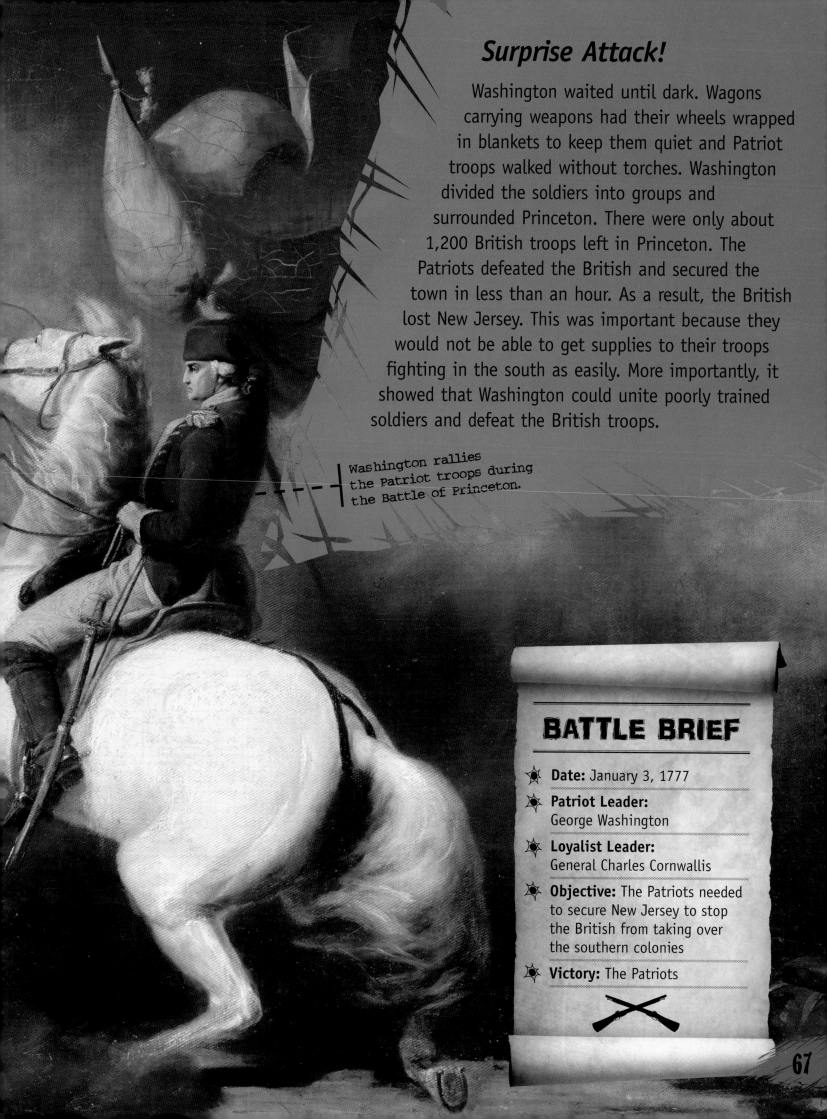

## Surprise Attack!

Washington waited until dark. Wagons carrying weapons had their wheels wrapped in blankets to keep them quiet and Patriot troops walked without torches. Washington divided the soldiers into groups and surrounded Princeton. There were only about 1,200 British troops left in Princeton. The Patriots defeated the British and secured the town in less than an hour. As a result, the British lost New Jersey. This was important because they would not be able to get supplies to their troops fighting in the south as easily. More importantly, it showed that Washington could unite poorly trained soldiers and defeat the British troops.

Washington rallies the Patriot troops during the Battle of Princeton.

## BATTLE BRIEF

☀ **Date:** January 3, 1777

☀ **Patriot Leader:** George Washington

☀ **Loyalist Leader:** General Charles Cornwallis

☀ **Objective:** The Patriots needed to secure New Jersey to stop the British from taking over the southern colonies

☀ **Victory:** The Patriots

# WEAPONS TECHNOLOGY

Long periods of warfare usually see improvements to existing weapons, or the development of something completely new, as each side tries to gain an advantage over the other.

## The Long Rifle

Developed in the first part of the 18th century, the long **rifle**, or Kentucky rifle, had spiraled grooves inside the barrel, which made the bullet spin as it was fired. This made it more accurate and gave it a greater range. However, the rifle was slower to load than a **flintlock** musket, which made it inappropriate for open battle.

Its accuracy made the long rifle ideal for individual snipers.

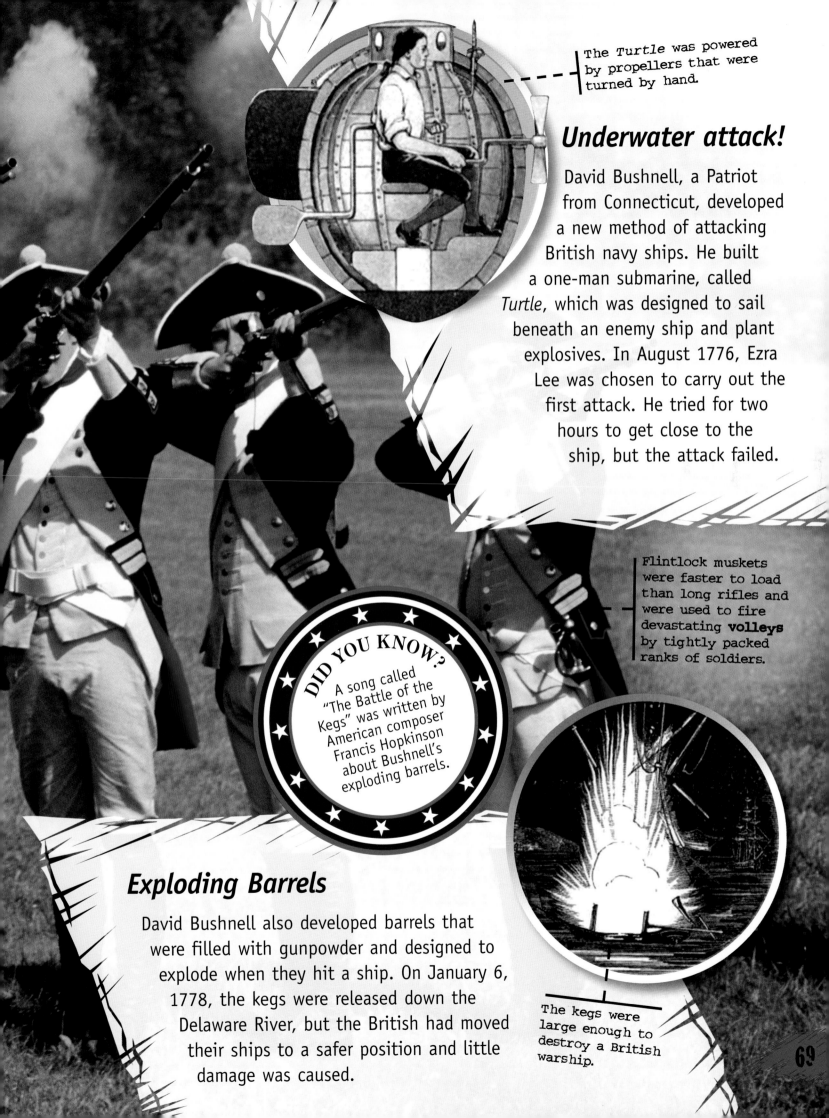

The *Turtle* was powered by propellers that were turned by hand.

## Underwater attack!

David Bushnell, a Patriot from Connecticut, developed a new method of attacking British navy ships. He built a one-man submarine, called *Turtle*, which was designed to sail beneath an enemy ship and plant explosives. In August 1776, Ezra Lee was chosen to carry out the first attack. He tried for two hours to get close to the ship, but the attack failed.

Flintlock muskets were faster to load than long rifles and were used to fire devastating **volleys** by tightly packed ranks of soldiers.

**DID YOU KNOW?**
A song called "The Battle of the Kegs" was written by American composer Francis Hopkinson about Bushnell's exploding barrels.

## Exploding Barrels

David Bushnell also developed barrels that were filled with gunpowder and designed to explode when they hit a ship. On January 6, 1778, the kegs were released down the Delaware River, but the British had moved their ships to a safer position and little damage was caused.

The kegs were large enough to destroy a British warship.

# AFRICAN– AMERICAN SOLDIERS

African-Americans took many different roles during the American Revolution. In northern colonies, slavery was less common and many slaves joined state militias. In the middle and southern colonies, however, many slaves sided with the Loyalists, hoping to gain their freedom.

## Becoming Involved

Between 15,000 and 100,000 African-Americans left their masters and fought with the British. Captain Tye was a Loyalist and well-known for his bravery. He commanded a group who raided Patriot homes and attacked Patriots who were known for killing Loyalists.

## The Chasseurs-Volontaires

In 1779, Saint-Domingue was a colony of France. It is now known as Haiti and the Dominican Republic. About 550 men from Saint-Domingue fought in the Revolutionary War on behalf of France. It was the largest unit of African soldiers to fight in the war. They were inexperienced soldiers, but brave.

A statue honoring the Chasseurs-Volontaires in Savannah, Georgia.

## After the War

When Britain lost the war, British General Guy Carleton insisted that African-American soldiers be set free. He had promised them freedom in exchange for their service. This angered George Washington, who insisted that they were stolen property. Most slaves would not find freedom until slavery was abolished in the United States in 1865.

At the end of the war, General Carleton helped more than 3,000 **freedmen** escape from New York.

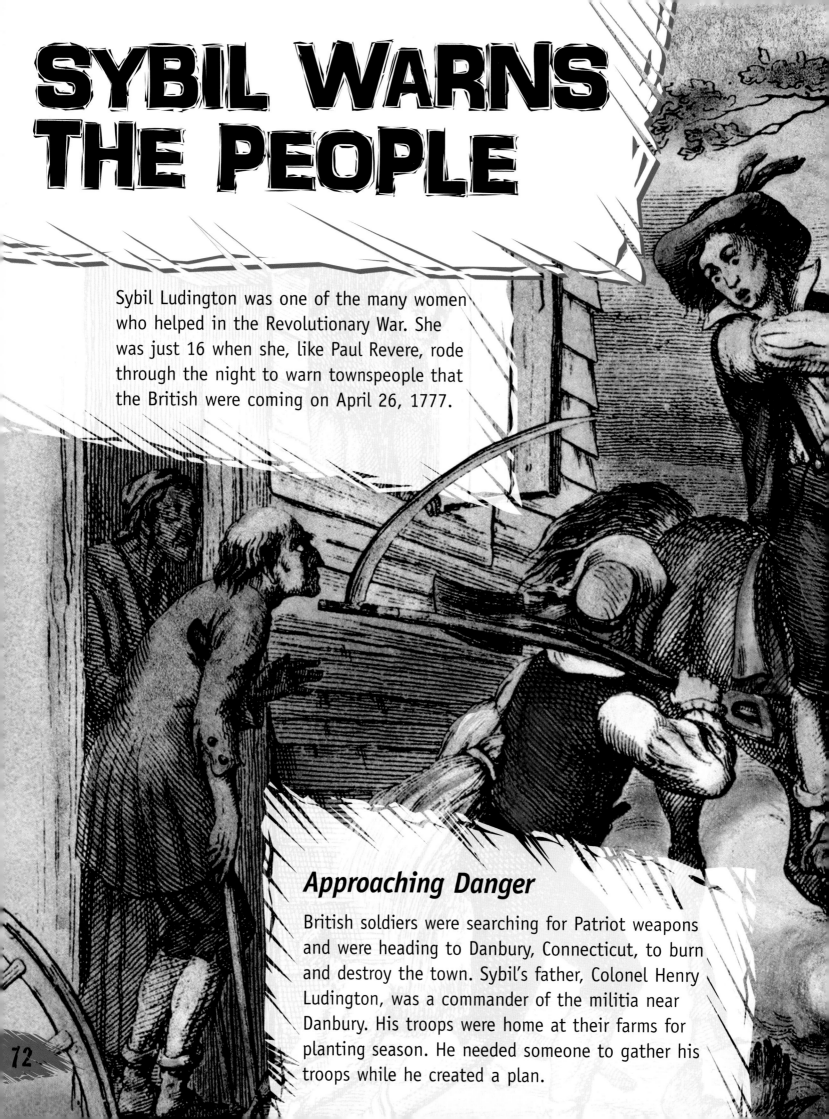

# SYBIL WARNS THE PEOPLE

Sybil Ludington was one of the many women who helped in the Revolutionary War. She was just 16 when she, like Paul Revere, rode through the night to warn townspeople that the British were coming on April 26, 1777.

## *Approaching Danger*

British soldiers were searching for Patriot weapons and were heading to Danbury, Connecticut, to burn and destroy the town. Sybil's father, Colonel Henry Ludington, was a commander of the militia near Danbury. His troops were home at their farms for planting season. He needed someone to gather his troops while he created a plan.

## Sybil's Ride

Colonel Ludington's daughter, Sybil, was an excellent rider and she knew the local dirt roads well. Though barely 16, she agreed to help her father. Sybil left in the dark to begin a 40-mile ride to gather his troops. It was cold and raining, but she returned home before daybreak unharmed.

Sybil rode 40 miles in the dark and rain to warn the people.

**DID YOU KNOW?**

Sybil's ride was almost twice the distance of Paul Revere's. George Washington visited Sybil to thank her for her bravery.

This statue of Sybil Ludington was made by Anna Hyatt Huntington and stands in Carmel, New York.

## Too Late!

The men she gathered were too late to save the town of Danbury. The British soldiers set homes and buildings ablaze, and stole anything they could. The militia was able to catch up with some British troops and fire at them, making their retreat difficult.

# THE BATTLE OF ORISKANY

**KEY**
- Patriot forces
- Loyalist forces

To Fort Stanwix

Loyalist troops attacked the supply column from both sides.

Native peoples were split in their support during the Revolutionary War. Many, like the Iroquois and Cherokees, supported the Loyalists. Battles involving native groups were mostly in western New York and Pennsylvania.

## Chief Thayendanegea

Thayendanegea was a Mohawk chief, also known as Joseph Brant. He conducted many raids against the Patriots in an effort to protect Iroquois country, and to prevent colonists from getting supplies. He also helped in the Battle of Oriskany.

Joseph Brant was the most influential Iroquois leader during the Revolutionary War.

# The Battle

Colonial Patriots in Fort Stanwix, New York, were surrounded by British soldiers. General Herkimer was bringing supplies and soldiers to help them. They were ambushed by Loyalists, including Joseph Brant and his men. It was one of the deadliest fights in the war. A powerful storm stopped the fighting briefly, allowing both sides to withdraw.

General Herkimer tries to organise his troops during the ambush.

Hand-to-hand fighting was fierce when Loyalists and Native Americans attacked the Patriots.

## BATTLE BRIEF

- **Date:** August 6, 1777
- **Patriot Leader:** General Nicholas Herkimer
- **Loyalist Leader:** Colonel Larry St. Leger
- **Objective:** General Herkimer was attempting to bring supplies to colonial soldiers at Fort Stanwix, which was surrounded by British troops
- **Victory:** Undecided

### DID YOU KNOW?

In total, 385 Patriot soldiers and their Native American allies were killed during the Battle of Oriskany.

# THE FALL OF FORT TICONDEROGA

Fort Ticonderoga had been captured by Ethan Allen and Benedict Arnold early in the revolution. Now the British wanted to take it back. The British soldiers had help from the Hessians, Canadians, and Native American troops to ensure a victory.

**KEY**
- Patriot forces
- Loyalist forces

Fort Ticonderoga

Lake Champlain

## The Plan

Fort Ticonderoga sat on a key position near Canada, and the British were determined to retake it. Under the command of General Burgoyne, Loyalist soldiers crept into position around the fort and the surrounding hills. The Patriots inside the fort could see that their position was hopeless, so they decided to evacuate.

The British planned to surround and bombard the fort.

## Leaving Ticonderoga

The colonists planned to take the weapons and supplies with them as they fled. However, some soldiers were not told of the plan and set fire to their rooms, destroying property so the Loyalists couldn't use it. The Loyalist soldiers saw the fire and realized the colonists were planning to escape.

General Burgoyne talks to Native American allies before the attack.

**DID YOU KNOW?**

In 1776, Benedict Arnold equipped many of the ships for the first American Navy with weapons from Fort Ticonderoga.

## The Result

Some Patriots managed to escape, but most were trapped and either killed or taken prisoner. King George III believed the fort was so important that when he heard the news, he thought he had won the whole war. Burgoyne was pleased with the win, though some British officers believed he let too many of the enemy get away.

## BATTLE BRIEF

- **Date:** July 2–5, 1777
- **Patriot Leader:** Major General Arthur St. Claire
- **Loyalist Leader:** General John Burgoyne, using Hessian soldiers, as well as Canadian and Native American troops
- **Objective:** The British wanted to reclaim Fort Ticonderoga
- **Victory:** The Loyalists

# THE BATTLE OF BENNINGTON

British troops under General Burgoyne were heading south, but running low on supplies. They planned an attack on Bennington, Vermont, to steal weapons and food. Colonists learned of the plan and started heading toward Bennington.

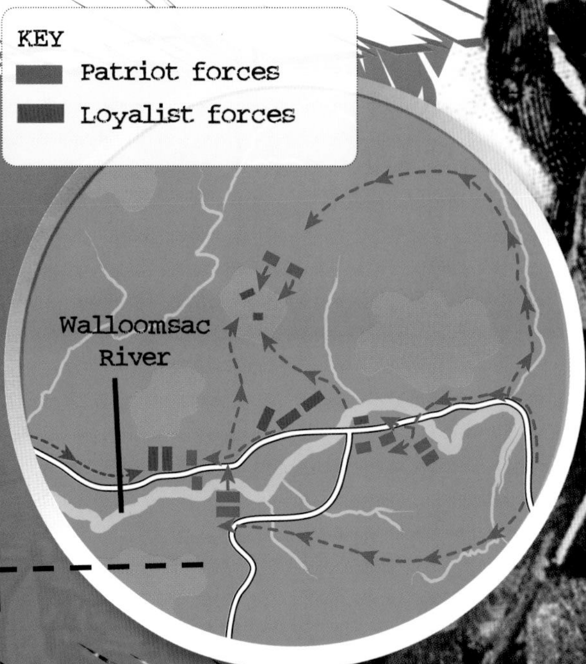

Patriot troops were almost successful in surrounding the Loyalist forces.

**KEY**
- Patriot forces
- Loyalist forces

Walloomsac River

**DID YOU KNOW?**
Loyalist forces included Canadians, Native Americans, Germans, and British. They spoke different languages and had trouble understanding one another.

## The Attack

The militia had more fighters than the Loyalists, who lined up ready to fight. The Loyalists also didn't realize that General Stark and the militiamen were surrounding them until it was too late. The Patriots began shooting, and Colonel Baum was killed. After more fighting, the British eventually retreated.

**BATTLE BRIEF**

- **Date:** August 6–16, 1777
- **Patriot Leaders:** General John Stark, Seth Warner, Vermont militia
- **Loyalist Leaders:** General John Burgoyne, Lieutenant Colonel Friedrich Baum
- **Objective:** The British wanted to destroy Bennington, and take any weapons and supplies
- **Victory:** The Patriots

Patriot militiamen storm British positions during the battle.

Patriot soldiers lead away Loyalist prisoners of war after the Battle of Bennington.

## The Result

The biggest problem for General Burgoyne was the lost troops. His lack of troops threatened his push south and he was unable to steal the supplies his men desperately needed. On the other side, the Patriots' confidence increased. It also encouraged more men to join the militia and showed how important they could be to the Patriot cause.

79

# THE BATTLE OF BRANDYWINE

Philadelphia, Pennsylvania, was the capital of the colonies at the time and capturing the city could win the war for the Loyalists. Washington placed troops along the Brandywine River. He thought that would stop British troops from reaching Philadelphia.

General Howe knew of an unguarded river crossing he could use to surprise the Patriots.

Brandywine creek

**KEY**
Patriot forces
Loyalist forces

## The Battle

It was a very foggy morning, which made spotting the enemy difficult. Washington received conflicting reports about British troop movements and this added to the confusion. The British crossed the river without a problem and nearly surrounded the Continental Army. Washington realized he would not be able to defend Philadelphia.

**DID YOU KNOW?** Among the Patriot fighters was Frenchman Marquis de Lafayette. He would later prove vital in persuading France to join the war on the Patriot side.

## Knowing Your Enemy

The British went on to capture Philadelphia, and Congress was forced to escape to York, Pennsylvania, taking military supplies with them. The Patriots learned the importance of knowing the landscape and of spying on enemy troops.

The Patriots had to put up a fierce defense to stop the British from wiping out their entire army.

### BATTLE BRIEF

☀ **Date:** September 11, 1777

☀ **Patriot Leader:**
George Washington

☀ **Loyalist Leader:**
General Sir William Howe

☀ **Objective:** The British wanted to capture Philadelphia, the capital of the colonies

☀ **Victory:** The Loyalists

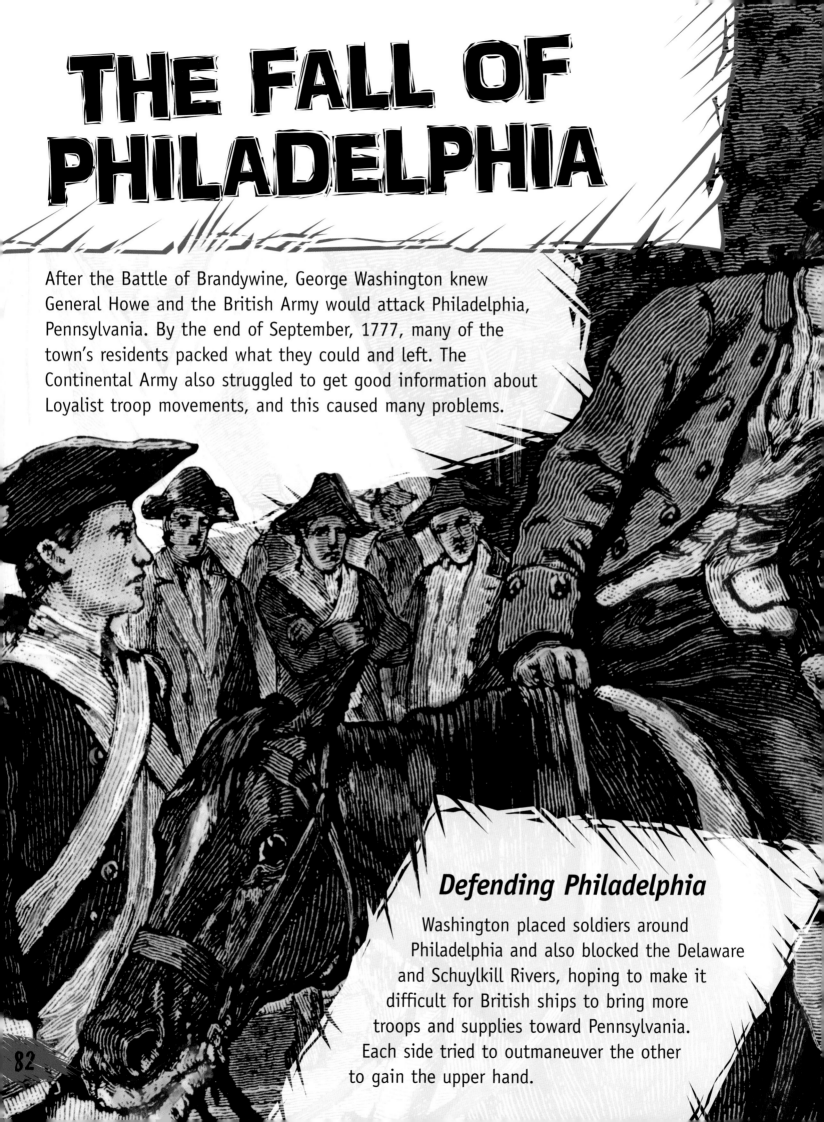

# THE FALL OF PHILADELPHIA

After the Battle of Brandywine, George Washington knew General Howe and the British Army would attack Philadelphia, Pennsylvania. By the end of September, 1777, many of the town's residents packed what they could and left. The Continental Army also struggled to get good information about Loyalist troop movements, and this caused many problems.

## Defending Philadelphia

Washington placed soldiers around Philadelphia and also blocked the Delaware and Schuylkill Rivers, hoping to make it difficult for British ships to bring more troops and supplies toward Pennsylvania. Each side tried to outmaneuver the other to gain the upper hand.

## Taking the City

After a number of clashes between the two sides, General Howe succeeded in moving around Patriot forces and was able to march into Philadelphia and capture the city. However, fighting continued in Philadelphia for more than a month and much of the city was destroyed in the violence.

Washington hears that the British have taken Philadelphia.

### DID YOU KNOW?

The Liberty Bell was taken to Allentown, Pennsylvania, on September 23, 1777, in order to keep it safe. It didn't return until June 27, 1778.

FREEDOM IS A LIGHT
WHICH MANY MEN HAVE DIED IN DA

MARKED GRAVES WITHIN
SQUARE LIE THOUSANDS
UNKNOWN SOLDIERS OF
ASHINGTON'S ARMY WHO DIED
WOUNDS AND SICKNESS DURING
THE REVOLUTIONARY WAR

THE INDEPENDENCE AND LIBE
YOU POSSESS ARE THE WORK
JOINT COUNCILS AND JOINT
EFFORTS OF COMMON DANGERS
SUFFERINGS AND SUCCESS
WASHINGTON'S FAREWELL ADDRESS SEPT 17, 1796

## Not the End

Even though the Loyalists had succeeded in capturing the Patriot capital city, they hadn't defeated the enemy. The Patriots continued fighting and the Loyalists were forced to abandon Philadelphia in June 1778.

Thousands of soldiers on both sides died in Philadelphia during the war. They are honored with this memorial.

# REVOLUTIONARY SPIES

Because there were no phones or computers, finding information about the enemy was difficult. Many brave people put their lives in danger to spy on the enemy. Any spies who were caught were usually hanged.

Lydia Darragh passes on information to a rider to take back to Patriot **headquarters**.

## Nathan Hale

Hale was an officer in the Continental Army, but before the war he had been a teacher. George Washington asked for volunteers to collect **intelligence** early in the war. This meant working behind enemy lines to discover Loyalist plans. Hale posed as a teacher and gathered information on the enemy. He was caught just before he could return home and he was hanged.

Hale walks to his execution on September 22, 1776.

## Women Spies

Women were not allowed to fight in the war, and men rarely paid attention to them. Some women, including Dicey Langston and Lydia Darragh, took advantage of this. They listened to the conversations of soldiers and shared information that might be helpful to the other side. Other women were used to carry secret messages, and could walk past enemy soldiers without raising suspicion.

Dicey Langston is said to have protected her father from Loyalists by standing in front of their weapons.

## Secret Messages

Codes were used to sneak messages past enemy patrols. That way if the message was read by the enemy, they wouldn't realize the importance of the note. Invisible ink could be made by mixing a chemical called ferrous sulfate with water. When the paper was exposed to heat, or another chemical, the actual note would be revealed. Letters were also sent inside secret containers, such as the inside of a hollow quill.

Some spy codes used numbers to represent people or phrases.

# BATTLE OF GERMANTOWN

With Philadelphia under British control, General Howe kept his troops at nearby Germantown. However, it was not well defended and Washington hoped to attack the British and regain control of the town.

Washington planned to divide his force into four groups and surround the British.

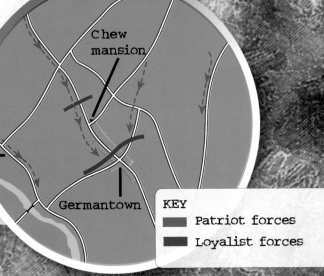

Chew mansion

Germantown

**KEY**
- Patriot forces
- Loyalist forces

## BATTLE BRIEF

✸ **Date:** October 4, 1777

✸ **Patriot Leaders:** George Washington, General Nathanael Greene

✸ **Loyalist Leader:** General Sir William Howe

✸ **Objective:** George Washington wanted to attack British soldiers who were staying there after winning Philadelphia

✸ **Victory:** The Loyalists

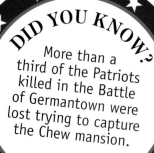

**DID YOU KNOW?**
More than a third of the Patriots killed in the Battle of Germantown were lost trying to capture the Chew mansion.

## The Battle

A thick morning fog caused confusion on the battlefield. The battle started well for the Patriots, but they became bogged down in attacking the Chew mansion, inside of which many British soldiers had taken shelter. This cost the Patriots vital men and ammunition. Communication between the four Patriot groups broke down. Two American groups, one under Anthony Wayne and the other under Nathanael Greene, even started shooting at each other. With losses mounting, Washington was forced to order a withdraw.

Washington set up his headquarters in this building.

Washington made several costly attempts to capture the Chew mansion.

The Patriot group under Nathanael Greene arrived late to the battle.

## The Result

The Patriots were severely beaten and many of Washington's men were killed. Other leaders in the Continental Army started to question Washington's ability to lead them to victory.

# BATTLES OF SARATOGA

General Burgoyne continued his march south and hoped to meet up with another Loyalist force from the south. However, this other force did not appear, and Burgoyne had to face two battles with Patriot forces near Saratoga, New York.

The two battles took place 18 days apart.

Freeman's Farm

Bemis Heights

Hudson River

**KEY**
- Patriot forces
- Loyalist forces

## The Battle at Freeman's Farm

The first battle took place at Freeman's Farm on September 19, 1777. General Burgoyne's men had more artillery, but the Patriots were better shots and managed to kill many British officers and artillerymen. As darkness approached, the Patriots retreated from the battlefield, leaving the Loyalists victorious.

Patriot forces were led by General Horatio Gates.

## The Second Battle

Burgoyne was waiting for more British soldiers to arrive, but they were slow in coming. He decided to attack at Bemis Heights on October 7. The Patriot response was fierce and they drove Loyalist troops back. Burgoyne was forced to retreat to Saratoga, where he was surrounded by Patriot troops. He surrendered his army on October 17.

**DID YOU KNOW?**

With the surrender of Burgoyne's army after the Battles of Saratoga, the Loyalists lost more than 7,000 soldiers.

Benedict Arnold led several brave charges during the second battle and was wounded when his horse fell on him.

## The Result

The Battles of Saratoga were a major turning point in the war. While the men were fighting in North America, Benjamin Franklin was in France convincing King Louis XVI to help the American cause. These battles helped to persuade the French that the Americans truly wanted independence. The French king decided to help.

## BATTLE BRIEF

- **Date:** September 19 and October 7, 1777
- **Patriot Leaders:** Horatio Gates and Benedict Arnold
- **Loyalist Leader:** General John Burgoyne
- **Objective:** General Burgoyne was moving his troops to capture the southern colonies
- **Victory:** The Patriots

# BRITISH MILITARY LEADERS

In order to win the war, Britain sent many of its best military officers to North America to try to keep the colonies under British control.

Patriot leaders accept the surrender of British troops after the defeat at Saratoga.

## General Burgoyne

Following his surrender at Saratoga, General Burgoyne was sent back to Britain in disgrace. The British king even refused to meet him when he returned. Some people think he should have been held captive in America as a prisoner of war.

**DID YOU KNOW?**

After the war, John Burgoyne became a celebrated author writing several plays as well as the words for an opera.

## Lord Cornwallis

Charles Cornwallis led British troops to many victories early in the war. However, he was forced to surrender at the Battle of Yorktown. Unlike Burgoyne, he was still well liked after the end of the war and he was made Governor of India.

Cornwallis was a member of the British Parliament and he voted against the Stamp Act.

Howe was criticized back in Britain for not helping Burgoyne enough.

## William Howe

William Howe joined the Loyalist forces in May 1775. He helped win the Battle of Bunker Hill, but lost a lot of men doing so. As a result, he became more careful about sending his troops into battle. He eventually became commander of the British Army. He was victorious in the Battle of Long Island in August 1776, but he was still careful with his soldiers. Many times Patriots escaped before Howe made the decision to attack them. He resigned his command in 1778.

# ARTICLES OF CONFEDERATION

Having declared themselves independent, the Patriots needed a **constitution** to say how they were going to be governed. Completed on November 15, 1777, a document called the Articles of Confederation was the first attempt at writing such a constitution.

## The Purpose

The articles outlined a union of all the colonies. They gave power to the Continental Congress, allowing them to make decisions. These included declaring war, making war strategies, and negotiating with other countries. Congress would also have the power to solve any problems between states.

John Dickinson, a member of Congress from Philadelphia, was the key writer for the first draft.

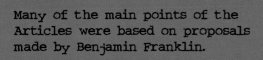

Many of the main points of the Articles were based on proposals made by Benjamin Franklin.

## Concerns

Many states did not agree with the Articles of Confederation. These states wanted to make sure that Congress would only try to solve problems that the individual states could not solve themselves.

## Raising Taxes

The Continental Congress became "The United States in Congress Assembled" on March 2. One of the most important topics debated during that first meeting was taxes to raise money so that the Continental Army had supplies. The Articles of Confederation lasted until the Federal Constitution took over in 1788.

The Second Continental Congress drafted and signed the Articles of Confederation in York, Pennsylvania, on November 15, 1777.

The York County Courthouse where the document was drafted.

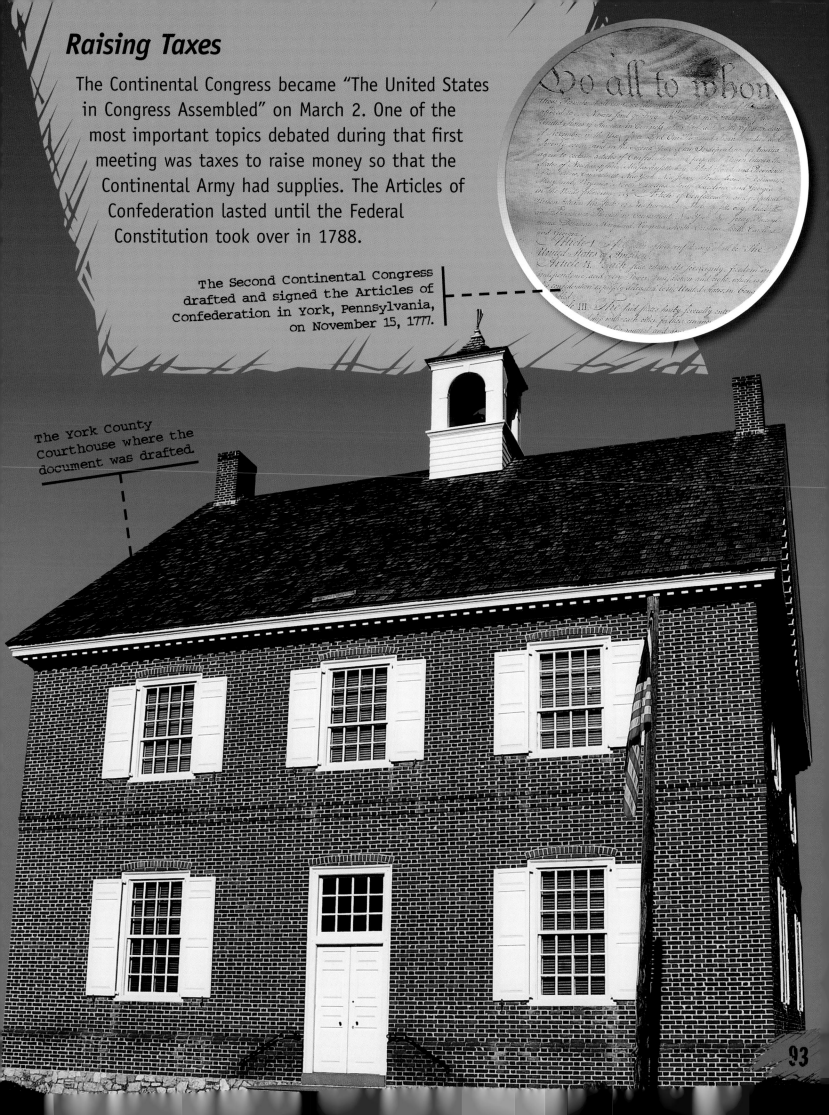

93

# VALLEY FORGE

By December 1777, the Continental Army was tired and frustrated. They had won at Saratoga, but lost the battles of Brandywine and Germantown. More importantly, they had lost Philadelphia. Many men wanted to quit, but Washington encouraged them to stay.

**DID YOU KNOW?**
Troops who were familiar with cold winters dug three-foot pits before building their huts. This offered protection from the wind.

## Exhausted Patriots

Washington took 11,000 troops to Valley Forge, Pennsylvania, for the winter. The camp was close to Philadelphia so they could keep watch on the British soldiers but far enough away that they were unlikely to be attacked.

Many of the Patriot soldiers marched to Valley Forge with their clothes in tatters and no shoes on their feet.

94

## Shortages

The men lacked many things. There were no blankets or meat. By Christmas, even the flour was running low. The men didn't have soap and couldn't get clean. This resulted in lice and disease. They built huts as best they could, but they were low on nails and tools. Snow and sleet made the work harder.

Huts measured 12 by 16 feet, and were 6 feet high. Twelve men slept in each hut.

## Working Together

The troops came from all 13 states. Women and children followed their husbands to camp. In addition to English colonists, there were soldiers from Africa, Austria, France, Poland, and Spain, as well as many other countries. They took turns searching for food in the woods, though there was rarely enough to eat.

# FRANCE JOINS THE WAR

France was still upset following its loss to Britain in the French and Indian War. When the French learned that the colonists were fighting the British, they wanted to help. In 1776, France sent weapons to help the colonists fight the war. They also gave colonists money to pay for soldiers and the supplies they needed.

## Becoming Partners

To beat the British, however, the Patriots needed more help. Benjamin Franklin, Silas Deane, and Arthur Lee went to France on October 26, 1776, to try to persuade the French to become allies in the fight against the British.

Benjamin Franklin served as ambassador to France from 1776 to 1785.

## Persuading France

The Battles of Saratoga proved to France that the Patriots were committed to independence, so they decided to help. On February 6, 1778, France signed two **treaties** with the United States. The Treaty of Amity and Commerce recognized that the United States was an independent nation, and the two countries could trade items with each other. A Treaty of Alliance stated that the two countries were united against Britain.

Benjamin Franklin met with King Louis XVI in the hope of creating a formal alliance.

### DID YOU KNOW?

During the Revolutionary War, France fought battles against Britain in North America, the Caribbean, the Bay of Biscay, and India.

# SUPPLIES AND TRAINING

Back at Valley Forge, George Washington demanded that Congress supply the troops with food and clothing. He feared that without them, the soldiers would leave the army. He had to be careful though. If the British found out how bad things were, they would attack the Continental Army.

Washington toured the camp regularly to check on his soldiers.

**DID YOU KNOW?**
The alliance between France and America was signed in February 1778, but it took weeks for the news to reach Valley Forge.

Steuben taught the soldiers how to march, load and fire their weapons quickly, and how to use their bayonets.

## Visitors

Lieutenant General Steuben was a Prussian officer who volunteered to help the Continental Army. During the stay at Valley Forge, he worked hard to drill the troops, turning them into a military unit that could win the war. Washington's wife, Martha, also came to live at Valley Forge. She helped to distribute food and she also organized a sewing circle so that women in the camp could repair clothing.

Martha Washington visited troops in their huts to keep morale high.

## Starting to Improve

Very slowly, things at Valley Forge began to improve. Men sang and played music to keep themselves occupied, while others wrestled. Then the soldiers at Valley Forge learned that France had agreed to help them beat Britain. A day of celebration was held on May 6, 1778. The soldiers had a parade. It helped the men recognize that they now had uniforms and were an organized fighting unit. A cannon boomed thirteen times, once for each colony. They were now a trained, united force, ready to beat the British. Washington led the Continental Army out of Valley Forge on June 19, 1778.

99

# BATTLE OF MONMOUTH

With France's entry into the war, British leaders felt that the city of New York was under threat. They decided to abandon Philadelphia and move their troops north to fortify New York City.

The retreating Patriots were chased by British troops.

Monmouth Court House

KEY
Patriot forces
Loyalist forces

## *Chasing the British*

Washington decided to attack the British soldiers as they left Philadelphia and he sent a force under the command of General Charles Lee. He ordered General Lee to attack the British, while he brought more soldiers in for a second attack. However, Lee's attack near Monmouth Court House was disorganized and his troops retreated. When Washington caught up with Lee's men, he was angry that they were retreating. He organized the retreating soldiers to form a defense and stopped the British advance.

Washington had to rally the retreating Patriot soldiers to stop a crushing defeat.

## Washington gets tricked

Throughout the rest of the day, the two sides fought themselves to a standstill. As night started to fall, both leaders decided to stop fighting. Washington assumed the battle would begin again when the sun rose. As he prepared his troops the next morning, however, he discovered that the British had left in the middle of the night to continue their march north.

After the battle, General Lee was suspended from his position in the army.

## BATTLE BRIEF

- **Date:** June 28, 1778
- **Patriot Leader:** George Washington, General Charles Lee
- **Loyalist Leader:** General Sir Henry Clinton
- **Objective:** The Continental Army wanted to stop the British from returning to New York City
- **Victory:** Undecided

### DID YOU KNOW?

According to some accounts, heatstroke brought on by high temperatures caused more deaths than musket fire during the battle.

# WOMEN OF THE REVOLUTION

Instead of just staying at home, many women took an active part in the conflict. They followed their husbands into battle, performing vital roles and even fighting.

## Margaret Cochran Corbin

Corbin's husband, John, was a cannon loader in the Continental Army. Margaret followed her husband during the war, cooking and doing laundry in the camp and helping to care for sick and wounded soldiers. When John was killed during the Battle at Fort Washington on November 16, 1776, Margaret took his place operating the cannon until she was severely wounded and forced to surrender.

This memorial was built to honor Corbin after her death in 1800.

## Mary Ludwig

In the hot weather of the Battle of Monmouth, Mary Ludwig carried water to the thirsty Patriot soldiers. When her husband had to be taken away from the battlefield, Mary took his place, helping to operate the cannon he had been firing. Her bravery that day earned her the nickname "Molly Pitcher" and she was made a **non-commissioned officer** by George Washington himself.

During the battle, a British cannonball flew between Mary's legs without injuring her.

## Abigail Adams

Abigail Adams was married to John Adams, a member of Congress and Patriot leader. She cared for militiamen who came to her home. She also encouraged her husband to give women more freedoms than they currently had as he wrote the laws for the new country.

Abigail Adams became First Lady when her husband became President in 1797.

# THE LIFE OF A SOLDIER

A soldier's life could be very hard, especially when conditions were harsh and supplies were scarce.

## Food and Clothing

While at base or camp, soldiers could receive good supplies of food and clothing. But when they were on the march, they often had to make do with what they could scavenge. At the end of a long campaign, soldiers could be starving and their clothes ragged from many weeks in the field.

A Patriot soldier in a ragged uniform.

## Accommodation

Soldiers mostly lived in tents. British tents were about six feet high and seven feet long and slept five men. Officers had larger tents where they could meet and discuss plans, or they would take over a nearby house to make their **headquarters**.

Patriot prisoners endured terrible conditions aboard prison ships.

## Disease

Living in filthy conditions while eating a poor diet meant that many diseases were common in the life of a Revolutionary War soldier. Conditions were particularly bad aboard the ships the British used to house prisoners of war. Common diseases during the conflict included smallpox, malaria, and dysentery. It's said that the Patriots lost more men to disease than to the enemy.

Patriot soldiers try to keep warm during the winter at Valley Forge.

105

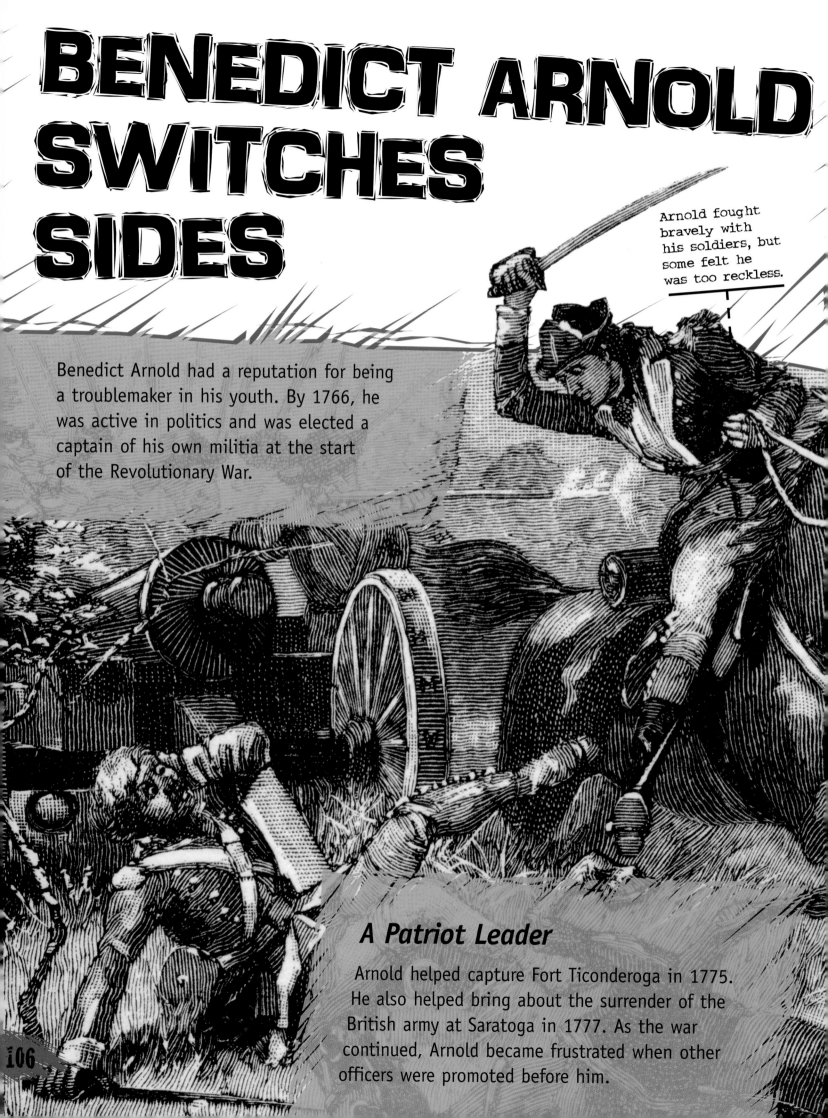

# BENEDICT ARNOLD SWITCHES SIDES

Arnold fought bravely with his soldiers, but some felt he was too reckless.

Benedict Arnold had a reputation for being a troublemaker in his youth. By 1766, he was active in politics and was elected a captain of his own militia at the start of the Revolutionary War.

## A Patriot Leader

Arnold helped capture Fort Ticonderoga in 1775. He also helped bring about the surrender of the British army at Saratoga in 1777. As the war continued, Arnold became frustrated when other officers were promoted before him.

## Bad Reputation

While a good officer, Arnold had a reputation for disobeying commands, as well as having a bad temper. He believed he deserved more credit than he was given. In August 1779, Arnold was given command of the base at West Point, New York, one of the most important posts in America at the time.

Benedict Arnold is remembered both as a traitor and as an excellent military commander.

### DID YOU KNOW?

West Point was near New York City on the Hudson River. If the British took control of it, they would have split the 13 colonies into two parts.

## Changing Sides

Arnold felt he should have been given a bigger role in the Continental Army. He began talking to the Loyalists. He planned to give West Point over to the British. His plan was discovered, and he escaped on a British ship on September 25, 1780. The British made him a brigadier general in their army.

John Andre was a British spy who persuaded Arnold to switch sides. He was caught and hanged on October 2, 1780.

# ATTACKING SAVANNAH

The British captured Savannah, Georgia, in 1778, and the Patriots were keen to retake the city with the help of their new French allies.

The Loyalists built huge defenses around the city.

Savannah

Savannah River

**KEY**
- Patriot forces
- Loyalist forces

A replica of one of the ships used to transport French troops.

## The French Arrive

French warships started to land soldiers near Savannah in September 1779. However, Loyalist troops and engineers had built an enormous chain of ditches and walls to protect the city. The French started to bombard the city, rather than these defenses.

## On the Attack

After five days of bombardment, the French decided to attack the Loyalist positions. However, the defenses were too strong, and wave after wave of attacking troops were beaten back in one of the bloodiest battles of the war. Eventually, the Patriots and French were forced to give up and retreat.

# BATTLE BRIEF

* **Date:** September–October 1779
* **Patriot Leaders:** Count Charles Henri d'Estaing of France, Arthur Dillon, and Casimir Pulaski
* **Loyalist Leaders:** Colonel Campbell and Lieutenant colonel John Maitland
* **Objective:** To re-take Savannah and stop Loyalist forces from conquering the southern colonies
* **Victory:** The Loyalists

French troops attack the Loyalist defenses during the siege.

**DID YOU KNOW?**
Loyalists assumed people in the south would be loyal to the king. When they tried to recruit new troops, they found out that they were wrong.

## The Result

Some Americans were frustrated that the French army was unable to secure a victory in battle. The Loyalists were excited about their success and they hoped to conquer the rest of the south quickly.

# THE PATRIOTS LOSE CHARLESTON

Having succeeded in defeating the Patriot attack on Savannah, the Loyalists turned their attention to capturing Charleston, South Carolina. From here, they could push across the other southern colonies and knock them out of the war.

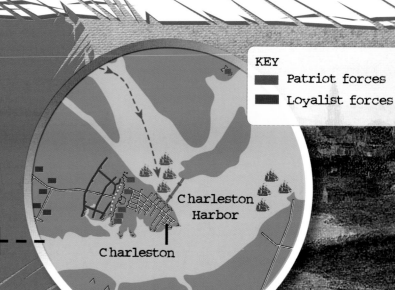

**KEY**
■ Patriot forces
■ Loyalist forces

Charleston Harbor

Charleston

The city was surrounded by British soldiers and ships.

## BATTLE BRIEF

☀ **Date:** March–May 1780

☀ **Loyalist Leader:** Major General Benjamin Lincoln

☀ **Patriot Leader:** Lieutenant General Sir Henry Clinton

☀ **Objective:** The Loyalists wanted to conquer the southern colonies

☀ **Victory:** The Loyalists

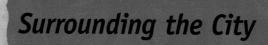

Loyalist troops bombard the Patriot positions in the city.

## Surrounding the City

The British navy brought soldiers to South Carolina in the spring of 1780. By April 1, they began surrounding Charleston and started to bombard the Patriot positions. The city was poorly prepared for such an attack and had very weak fortifications.

## Surrender

The government in South Carolina offered soldiers $500 and 100 acres of land to fight. If they served for 21 months they would receive $2,500 more. However, most militiamen chose to stay and protect their homes rather than fight the British. Also, the South Carolina government refused to allow slaves to fight. With so few men to defend the city, Charleston surrendered to the British on May 12, 1780. It was the worst defeat for the Patriots in the southern states, with a huge number of soldiers taken prisoner, along with their weapons and supplies.

Governor John Rutledge spent $5.4 million dollars ($89.2 million today) trying to defeat the British.

**DID YOU KNOW?**
Nearly 5,500 Patriot soldiers were taken prisoner. It remained the largest surrender of American soldiers until the Civil War almost 100 years later.

# BATTLE OF COWPENS

Patriot General Daniel Morgan knew his militiamen became nervous and were likely to run away during battle. He developed an ingenious plan to make the most of the militiamen in his force.

## A Cunning Plan

Morgan divided his men into four groups and gave them very specific instructions. The first group of militiamen was to fire two shots, but to aim at British officers. After that, they could retreat. Behind them, he placed another row of militia who would do the same. Behind that row, he placed a third row of his best soldiers who would stand against the advance. Meanwhile, his cavalry waited nearby.

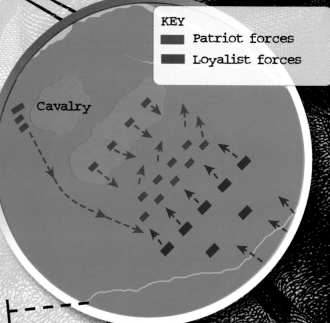

**KEY**
Patriot forces
Loyalist forces

Cavalry

The British were lured forward by the retreating Patriots.

## DID YOU KNOW?

The entire battle lasted just over an hour. At the end, more than 1,100 British soldiers had been killed, wounded, or captured.

## The Battle

The British commander Tarleton had forced his men to march a great distance to the battlefield in a very short time and many of them were exhausted. As the first two ranks of Patriots fired and withdrew, the British believed that they were winning and pushed on. However, they were brought to a standstill by the last group who didn't retreat. When the Patriots then fixed bayonets and charged and their cavalry appeared, the tired British troops ran away or quickly surrendered.

Cavalry troops clash at the Battle of Cowpens.

## The Result

The Battle of Cowpens slowed British progress across the south. It also proved to the American militiamen that if they stayed to fight rather than ran away, they could beat the British. General Tarleton returned in disgrace and wasn't trusted with the command of British troops again.

## BATTLE BRIEF

- **Date:** January 17, 1781
- **Patriot Leaders:** Lieutenant Colonel William Washington, Brigadier General Daniel Morgan
- **Loyalist Leader:** Lieutenant Colonel Banastre Tarleton
- **Objective:** The Patriots needed to stop the British from capturing the southern colonies
- **Victory:** The Patriots

# BATTLE OF THE CAPES

French and British warships fire at one another.

When he arrived in America, the French Admiral Comte de Grasse had a choice of attacking Loyalists in New York City or in Virginia. He chose to attack Virginia. Hearing this, General Washington changed his plans and moved his troops south to Virginia with the aim of surrounding the British army in Yorktown.

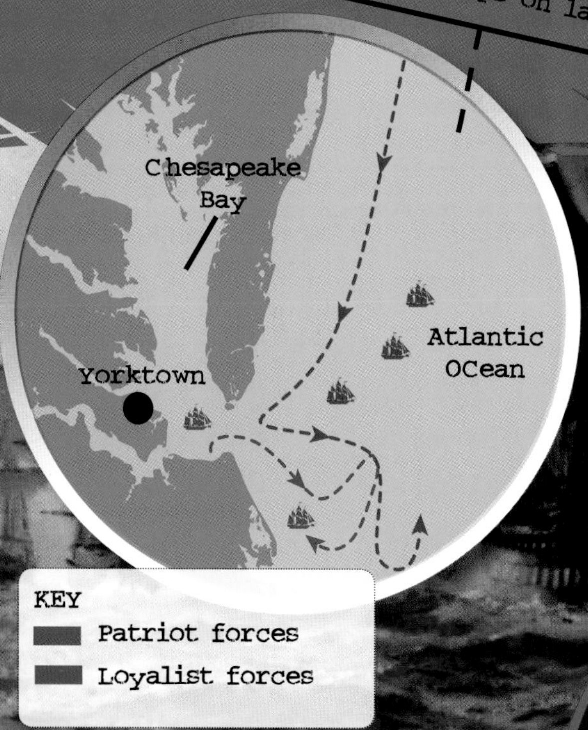

Controlling Chesapeake Bay would allow ships to supply troops on land.

Chesapeake Bay

Yorktown

Atlantic OCean

KEY
- Patriot forces
- Loyalist forces

**DID YOU KNOW?**
Washington knew how important a navy was. He said, "No land force can act decisively unless it is accompanied by **maritime** superiority."

## BATTLE BRIEF

⚜ **Date:** September 5, 1781

⚜ **Patriot Leader:**
Comte de Grasse of France

⚜ **Loyalist Leader:**
Admiral Thomas Graves

⚜ **Objective:** To get supplies to soldiers in Virginia, while preventing the enemy from doing so

⚜ **Victory:** The Patriots

## The Battle

The British fleet sailed to attack the French and both navies confronted each other. After two hours, the fighting stopped and British Admiral Graves and French Admiral De Grasse evaluated their ships. There was minor damage. The two sides then watched each other for days to see if the other would begin fighting again. When more French ships arrived, the British navy realized it could not defeat so many enemy ships and had to withdraw.

## The Result

The French Navy prevented British ships from entering the harbor and getting much-needed supplies to General Cornwallis and his troops in Yorktown. On the other hand, General Washington could use Chesapeake Bay to move troops and supplies to Yorktown. The Patriot victory at the Capes ensured a victory at Yorktown.

# BATTLE OF YORKTOWN

Once the British fleet had been defeated at the Battle of the Capes, General Cornwallis found himself trapped by French and American troops inside the city of Yorktown, Virginia.

French and American commanders give out orders during the siege.

**KEY**
- Patriot forces
- Loyalist forces

York River

Yorktown

The Loyalists were surrounded on both sides of the river.

## Tricking the Loyalists

Originally, Washington had planned to attack New York City, but he changed his mind when the French fleet sailed for Virginia. He marched south, but left some troops close to New York City to fool the Loyalists into thinking that he still wanted to attack there. Linking up with French troops, the Patriots took up positions around Yorktown.

## Bombardment

The French and American armies built fortified positions and started to fire on Loyalist troops. After many days of bombardment, the Patriots then attacked and took several key positions.

## BATTLE BRIEF

- **Date:** September–October 1781
- **Patriot Leaders:** George Washington, Comte de Rochambeau
- **Loyalist Leader:** General Charles Cornwallis
- **Objective:** To set up a siege and force the Loyalist troops trapped inside Yorktown to surrender, ending the war
- **Victory:** The Patriots

## DID YOU KNOW?

General Cornwallis claimed to be ill on the day of the surrender and he did not attend the official ceremony.

## Surrender

The Patriots were then able to bring up their cannons to these key positions. From here, the Loyalists would have little or no defense against the Patriot artillery. Cornwallis soon realized that his position was hopeless and, on October 19, Loyalist forces surrendered. The surrender of more than 7,500 Loyalist troops proved a decisive blow and led to the end of the war.

# THE WAR IS OVER

On November 25, 1781, King George III and the British parliament finally learned about the surrender at Yorktown. While the king was upset to lose the colonies, parliament accepted that the colonies were now independent. All the parties involved in the war met in Paris, France, to discuss peace terms and to sign a treaty.

Benjamin Franklin (right) discusses terms with the British representative Richard Oswald (left).

## Back in America

While the major battles had stopped, fighting still continued between Patriots and Loyalists, even though officers tried to stop it. Washington moved his men back to New York City to make sure the British did not try to recapture it. He left troops with General Greene in the south. The British had finally left the colonies by December 1782.

This painting of the signing parties of the Treaty of Paris remains unfinished because the British refused to sit for it.

## *The Treaty of Paris*

The Treaty of Paris was the formal document that officially ended the Revolutionary War and recognized American independence. John Adams, Benjamin Franklin, and John Jay from the Continental Congress signed the treaty on September 3, 1783. It was also signed by representatives from Britain, France, and Spain.

The last page of the treaty with the signatures and seals.

119

# WRITING THE CONSTITUTION

The Declaration of Independence was written in July 1776, and members of the Continental Congress wrote the Articles of Confederation in November 1777. Now a new document was needed to govern a new country.

Alexander Hamilton also founded the *New York Post* newspaper in 1801.

## Constitutional Convention

The states needed a stronger government after the war. Alexander Hamilton, an officer during the war, suggested that a Constitutional Convention meet to discuss these ideas. In May 1787, delegates from 12 of the states met to create a government and decide on its Constitution.

## Disagreements

Writing the Constitution was hard. Delegates argued about how much power the national government would have compared to the states. Many people wanted to make sure that states had their own rights. Slavery was another topic delegates disagreed on. Northern delegates were worried southern states wouldn't join the union if they outlawed slavery, so slavery was allowed.

The Constitution of the USA

Delegates debate the content of the Constitution.

**DID YOU KNOW?**

Rhode Island did not send a delegate to the Convention because they did not want a strong central government.

## Founding Fathers

It took several men to write the Constitution. Alexander Hamilton is credited for the idea. James Madison offered many ideas and is known as the "Father of the Constitution," while Thomas Jefferson and John Adams contributed ideas and revisions as well.

# RATIFYING AND THE BILL OF RIGHTS

Before the Constitution became law, it had to be approved, or **ratified**, by the states. Nine states needed to ratify the Constitution for it to come into effect. The delegates of the Constitutional Convention went to their home states to decide if they would vote for or against the Constitution.

**DID YOU KNOW?**
The Bill of Rights protected the citizens. It gave them rights to free speech, to protect themselves, and to have a fair trial.

Patrick Henry was governor of Virginia and a keen anti-federalist.

## For or Against?

Federalists supported the Constitution and thought it was essential to unite the states. Anti-federalists wanted the states to have more power. It took ten months for nine states to approve the Constitution, and it was not until 1790 that the last of the 13 states, Rhode Island, also agreed.

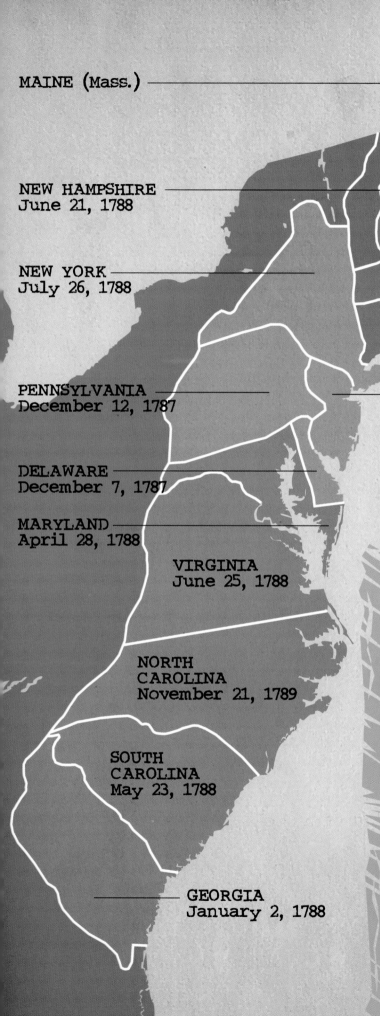

MAINE (Mass.)

NEW HAMPSHIRE
June 21, 1788

NEW YORK
July 26, 1788

PENNSYLVANIA
December 12, 1787

DELAWARE
December 7, 1787

MARYLAND
April 28, 1788

VIRGINIA
June 25, 1788

NORTH
CAROLINA
November 21, 1789

SOUTH
CAROLINA
May 23, 1788

GEORGIA
January 2, 1788

KEY

New England colonies
Middle colonies
Southern colonies

This map shows the dates
when each of the states
ratified the Constitution.

MASSACHUSETTS
February 6, 1788

RHODE ISLAND
May 29, 1790

CONNECTICUT
January 9, 1788

NEW JERSEY
December 18, 1787

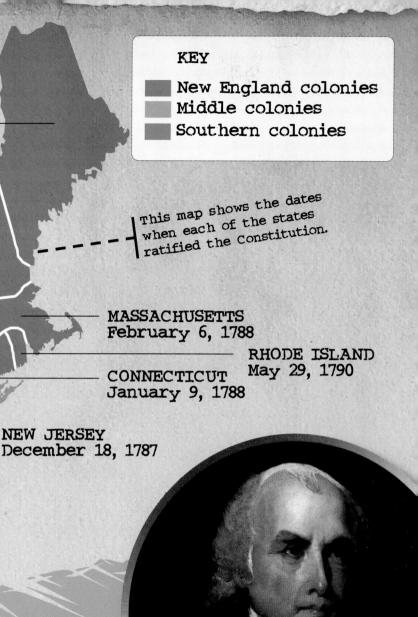

James Madison
became the fourth
President of the
United States.

## The Bill of Rights

James Madison knew that not every state
was happy with the Constitution. To try
to answer their concerns, he created ten
changes, or amendments, that became known
as the Bill of Rights. They were designed to
ensure certain freedoms for individual people
over the power of the federal government.

# THE FIRST PRESIDENT

George Washington became the first President of the United States on April 30, 1789. He took an oath of office at Federal Hall in New York City, the capital of the United States after the war.

**DID YOU KNOW?**
Some people criticized Washington for renting fine houses and being driven in a coach by four horses while he was President.

Washington owned a plantation at Mount Vernon, Virginia.

## The First President

George Washington had been commander of the colonial armies throughout the war. When the war ended, he went home to Mount Vernon. After the Constitution Convention, everyone agreed that Washington should be the first President. An election was held, and Washington received the most votes. John Adams became Vice President. Washington was President for two terms, from 1789 to 1797.

Washington was paid $25,000 a year while he was President.

## Shaping the Presidency

Washington knew he was setting an example for all future presidents. He chose Alexander Hamilton and Thomas Jefferson to help him. He made sure to listen to people before making decisions. He worked hard to unify and strengthen the new country.

John Adams was the first President to live in the White House we know today.

## Retirement

Some people wanted Washington to remain President. However, he decided being President for two terms was enough. It was important for America to have a peaceful change in government. John Adams was elected to be the second President in 1797. Washington died on December 14, 1799. His life was celebrated throughout the world as Americans mourned his death.

# AMERICA AFTER THE WAR

Once the Treaty of Paris was signed, America owned all the land between the Atlantic Ocean and the Mississippi River, and from the Great Lakes in the north to the 31st parallel in the south. The most significant change was the growth of the western frontier. This huge expansion of territory attracted new settlers who moved west in search of land to settle and develop.

**DID YOU KNOW?**

By the end of the 18th century, 200,000 settlers had migrated to Kentucky and Virginia, following routes marked out by Daniel Boone.

## *Pushing Back the Frontier*

One well-known frontiersman was Daniel Boone. He was a captain in the militia during the war. After the war, he was known for exploring throughout Kentucky and Missouri and creating settlements in those states. He often fought with native people over territory.

Daniel Boone leads a band of settlers west into the new territories.

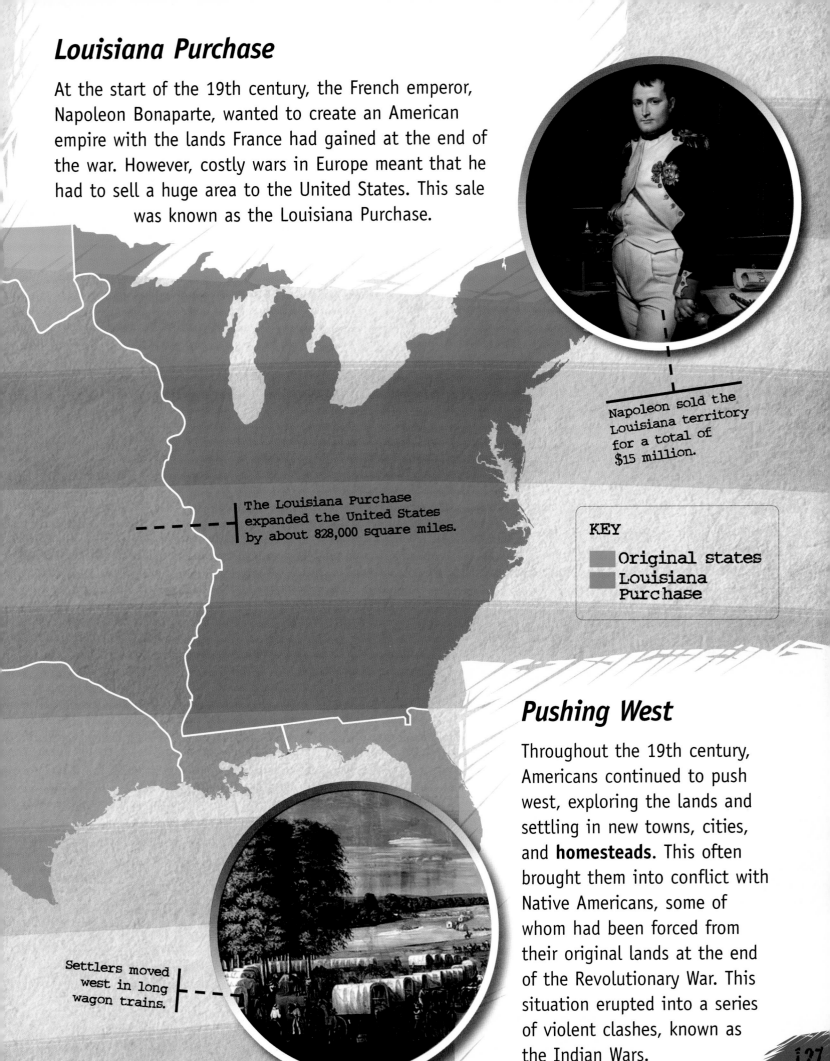

## Louisiana Purchase

At the start of the 19th century, the French emperor, Napoleon Bonaparte, wanted to create an American empire with the lands France had gained at the end of the war. However, costly wars in Europe meant that he had to sell a huge area to the United States. This sale was known as the Louisiana Purchase.

Napoleon sold the Louisiana territory for a total of $15 million.

The Louisiana Purchase expanded the United States by about 828,000 square miles.

**KEY**

◼ Original states
◼ Louisiana Purchase

## Pushing West

Throughout the 19th century, Americans continued to push west, exploring the lands and settling in new towns, cities, and **homesteads.** This often brought them into conflict with Native Americans, some of whom had been forced from their original lands at the end of the Revolutionary War. This situation erupted into a series of violent clashes, known as the Indian Wars.

Settlers moved west in long wagon trains.

# HEROES AND HEROINES

People from all walks of life were caught up in the events of the Revolutionary War. Many were directly involved in the fighting, while others acted secretly in the shadows. Some people were dragged into events by the actions of relatives or partners.

**DID YOU KNOW?**
Peggy Shippen followed her husband soon after he changed sides and they even moved to London. She and Arnold had five children together.

## Peggy Shippen Arnold

Peggy Shippen was married to Benedict Arnold. When Benedict Arnold became a traitor, people believed she was innocent. However, some historians now believe that she helped convince Arnold to change sides. Shippen had many Loyalist friends and she introduced Arnold to British officers. Soon after their wedding, Benedict Arnold began providing the British army with secret information. After the war, she was banned from Philadelphia. She died at age 44 from cancer on August 24, 1804.

Peggy Shippen spent days crying and screaming after her husband changed sides.

# Robert Townsend

Townsend was a member of the Culper Spy Ring and used the code name "Samuel Culper." He collected information about the British soldiers and was almost caught once, but managed to escape. He worked with Anna Strong, another spy. When Patriot spies had messages for Patriot leaders, Anna Strong would hang laundry on her clothesline. A black petticoat meant a message needed to be passed. White handkerchiefs on the clothesline would tell the spies where to meet.

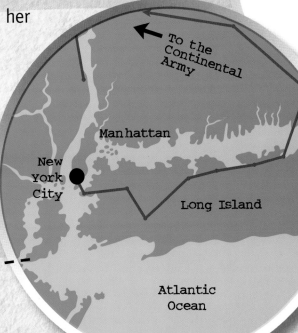

To the Continental Army

Manhattan

New York City

Long Island

Atlantic Ocean

To avoid being discovered, messages were taken on a long route from New York City to the Continental Army.

*Your humble servant*
*Robert Townsend*

The signature and silhouette of Culper Spy Ring member, Robert Townsend.

# Drummer Boy

Alexander Milliner was too young to fight in the Continental Army. Instead, he became a drummer boy. He also served in the navy during the War of 1812 against Britain. He died in 1865 at the age of 104, and was one of the last survivors of the Revolutionary War.

Drummers were used to send signals to the troops and to beat out rhythms they could march to.

# NATIVE PEOPLE, SLAVES, AND WOMEN

The Declaration of Independence said "all men are created equal." However, not all people were treated equally in the new country. It would take many years for all people to be protected equally under the laws.

President Abraham Lincoln signs the Emancipation Proclamation in January 1863, abolishing slavery.

## Slaves

In April 1776, Congress voted to stop the importing of slaves from Africa. Men like John Jay and Alexander Hamilton spoke out against slavery and many people joined anti-slavery groups. In 1804, all states north of Maryland and Delaware stopped slavery. Finally, in 1865, the 13th amendment was created, making slavery illegal.

Alexander Hamilton was a lifelong opponent of slavery.

## Native People

The war had a huge impact on native groups. Congress declared that any group who supported Britain should lose their lands. The Treaty of Paris gave America all the land between the Appalachian Mountains and the Mississippi River. Many Native Americans lived on that land, but now it belonged to the Americans. Native groups who helped the Americans, such as the Oneidas and Tuscaroras, were not rewarded for their work. Most native groups moved north and west in the hope of rebuilding their lives.

## Women

Women did not have many rights at the time of the revolution. A wife could not own her home or make money. Women could not sign contracts or vote. Some women, like Abigail Adams, began questioning women's rights. It would be decades before women began enjoying the same rights as men.

Elisabeth Cady Stanton (left) and Susan B. Anthony (right) fought for women's rights in the 19th century.

# TIMELINE

This timeline shows some of the key events that occurred during the Revolutionary War.

**October 26, 1774 Congress**
Meeting of the First Continental Congress.

**July 4, 1776 Independence**
America declares its independence.

**December 25–26, 1776 Battle of Trenton**
The Continental Army crosses the Delaware River.

**1774**

**1775**

**1776**

**1777**

**1778**

**April 18–19, 1775 Battle of Lexington and Concord**
The first shots of the American Revolution are fired.

**September–October, 1777 Battles of Saratoga**
The Patriots win.

**February 1778 France enters the war**
The French side with the Patriots

**June 16–17, 1775 Battle of Bunker Hill**
The Patriots lose, but fight well against the strong British army.

**December 1777–June 1778 Winter at Valley Forge**
The Continental Army is low on supplies and starving, but regroups and becomes stronger.

**June 28, 1778**
**Battle of Monmouth**
The Patriots attack British troops as they leave Philadelphia.

**September 5, 1781 Battle of the Capes**
The French and British fleets clash.

**September 25, 1780**
**Benedict Arnold**
Arnold switches sides and joins the British.

**October 19, 1781**
**Surrender at Yorktown**
The last major battle of the war.

1779   1780   1781   1782   1783   1784

**May 12, 1780**
**British take Charleston**
The British start attacking the southern colonies.

**January 17, 1781**
**Battle of Cowpens**
The Patriots win again.

**March 1, 1781**
**Articles**
The colonies adopt the Articles of Confederation.

**September 3, 1783**
**End of the war**
The Treaty of Paris formally ends the war.

# MONUMENTS

The first monument was built even before the Revolutionary War had ended. Today, hundreds of statues and memorials honor the bravery of men and women who acted for both sides during the conflict.

The monument was made in France and shipped to America in nine sealed cases with directions showing how to put it together.

## Montgomery Monument

The first monument was authorized by Congress in 1776. It honored Brigadier General Richard Montgomery who was killed in Quebec on December 31, 1775. It was placed at St. Paul's Chapel in New York City, where George Washington attended church.

# Crushing the Crown

The Boston Massacre and Crispus Attucks monument honors the victims of the Boston Massacre. It shows a figure representing the Spirit of the Revolution crushing the crown of the British king. It includes the names of the men killed before the war had even started.

Some people thought the monument was a bad idea because they felt the Patriots caused the massacre when they threw rocks at a British soldier.

The monument at Bunker Hill includes this statue of Patriot commander Colonel William Prescott.

**DID YOU KNOW?**
The Prison Ship Martyrs' Monument in Brooklyn, New York, is dedicated to the memory of more than 11,000 prisoners who died in the war.

# The Maryland 400

The Maryland 400 was a group of soldiers who made a brave stand against 2,000 British troops during the Battle of Long Island. Only a few of the Maryland 400 survived, but because of their bravery, George Washington was able to evacuate a large part of the Continental Army. Historians think that the soldiers who were killed are buried in a mass grave possibly under the streets of Brooklyn.

This memorial was built in honor of the Maryland 400.

# NATIONAL PARKS

As well as monuments honoring the dead, the U.S. government has set aside many areas where key events and battles took place during the Revolutionary War. These have been preserved as national parks.

## Concord

The Minute Man National Historical Park is located in Concord, Massachusetts. It's possible to walk the battlefields and explore the features associated with the battle. Each year on the anniversary of the battle, people reenact moments from the battle and teach visitors about this important Patriot victory.

Replicas of buildings from the period

## New York

Saratoga National Historical Park is in Stillwater, New York. Tourists can walk in the same woods where General Burgoyne's British army stood just before they surrendered to the Patriots. Visitors can also see the home of American General Philip Schuyler.

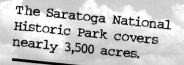

The Saratoga National Historic Park covers nearly 3,500 acres.

## Valley Forge

The Valley Forge National Historical Park is in Pennsylvania. Visitors can tour the place where the Continental Army spent the harsh winter of 1777–1778. They can see Washington's headquarters, as well as replicas of the wooden cabins the soldiers built and lived in.

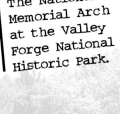

The National Memorial Arch at the Valley Forge National Historic Park.

## Yorktown

The Colonial National Historical Park in Yorktown, Virginia, is the site of the last major battle of the Revolutionary War. The park also preserves other sites relating to colonial Virginia, including the first English settlement of Jamestown.

Cannons line the path through the Yorktown battlefield site.

# CHANGES TO GOVERNMENT

Since the end of the Revolutionary War, Americans have made many changes to how they govern themselves. These include the founding of a new capital city, Washington, D.C., and alterations to the Constitution.

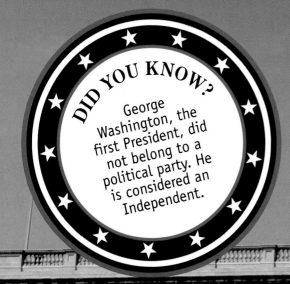

**DID YOU KNOW?**
George Washington, the first President, did not belong to a political party. He is considered an Independent.

Congress meets in the Capitol Building in Washington, D.C.

## Changes to the Constitution

In addition to the Bill of Rights, there have been a further 17 amendments made to the Constitution. They represented the changes in the United States of America. For example, the 13th amendment abolished, or ended, slavery, and the 19th amendment gave women the right to vote.

## Political Parties

The first political parties were the federalists and anti-federalists. Federalists believed the new central government should be stronger than the states, while anti-federalists wanted the opposite. Political parties have changed several times. Each political party has its own opinions about how America should be governed. The two biggest parties today are the Democrats and the Republicans. Because of the American Revolution, the Constitution, and the Bill of Rights, Americans have the right to choose which party they want to support.

The symbol for the Republican party is the elephant, while the Democratic symbol is the donkey.

The bald eagle is the national bird of the United States.

## Government Symbols

The Great Seal of the United States of America was created in 1782 and is still used today. It shows a bald eagle holding a scroll with a Latin phrase *E pluribus Unum*, meaning "one from many." This refers to the one nation created from 13 colonies. It can be seen on the back of the one-dollar bill. The eagle holds an olive branch and arrows, which are symbols for the power of peace and war.

# GLOSSARY

**Artillery** Large weapons that can fire heavy shells over a great distance.

**Bayonet** A long, sharp knife that can be fitted to the end of a firearm.

**Boycotting** Stopping the use or buying of goods or services.

**Chancellor of the Exchequer** The British minister who is responsible for looking after the economy.

**Coalition** A group of different people or countries that have joined together for a purpose.

**Colonies** Settlements that a country establishes and governs in a distant land.

**Colonists** People who live in colonies.

**Constitution** A set of rules and laws that state how a country will be governed.

**Continental Army** The name given to the formal Patriot army.

**Continental Congress** The name given to the group of Patriots who met to discuss how they should act against Britain.

**Continental Navy** The name given to the formal Patriot navy.

**Emigrants** People who leave one country and go to live in another.

**Empire** A collection of people, countries, and territories that are ruled by a single person, who is known as an emperor or empress.

**Fleet** A collection of ships and boats.

**Flintlock** A type of firearm that used a flint to create a spark to light the powder used to propel a lead shot.

**Fortifications** Walls and other defenses that are built to make a position hard to capture.

**Freedmen** People who have been freed from captivity or slavery.

**Governor** The chief politician in a region.

**Headquarters** The building or location from which military operations are directed.

**Hessian** The name given to German troops who were hired by the British.

**Homestead** The name given to a small-scale house and farm.

**Independent** Free to do what you want, without having to obey others.

**Intelligence** Information about an opponent's position or movements.

**Maritime** Something relating to the sea.

**Militia** An informal fighting force made up of citizens rather than professional soldiers.

**Minutemen** The name given to militiamen who could be ready to fight at a minute's notice.

**Musket** A long-barreled firearm that was loaded through the muzzle.

**Nomadic** Something or someone who moves around a lot and doesn't live in one spot.

**Non-commissioned officer** A rank of junior officer, such as a sergeant or a corporal.

**Parliament** A group of people who pass laws and govern a country.

**Plantations** A large estate where crops, such as cotton and tobacco, are grown.

**Prime Minister** The title given to the head of the British government.

**Propaganda** Information that is used to give one particular side of a story.

**Ranks** Rows of soldiers.

**Ratified** When something is formally approved.

**Rifle** A type of long-barreled firearm that has spiraled grooves carved into the barrel. These make a bullet spin so that it is more accurate and can travel farther.

**Royal Navy** The name of the British navy.

**Schooner** A type of sailing vessel which has at least two masts.

**Tarring and feathering** A form of punishment where a person is covered with hot, sticky tar and then covered with feathers.

**Tax** A sum of money that people have to pay. Taxes are usually imposed by a government to raise money to pay for services.

**Treaty** A formal agreement between several groups.

**Triangular Trade** The three-way trade between America, Europe, and Africa that saw raw materials being traded for manufactured goods and then slaves.

**Volley** The firing of several weapons at the same time.

# INDEX

# INDEX